MARRIAGE
the Way
God Intended

DR. NICOLE WITHERSPOON

ISBN 978-1-68570-857-3 (paperback)
ISBN 978-1-68570-858-0 (digital)

Christian Faith Publishing
832 Park Avenue
Meadville, PA 16335
www.christianfaithpublishing.com

Printed in the United States of America

In loving memory of my aunt, the late Glenda "Dee Dee" Mack (January 1, 1963–December 12, 2012). This book is dedicated to her husband/my uncle Leon Mack. Our families were always inspired by the twenty-eight years of marriage that you shared together from September 15, 1984, until Dee Dee's death on December 12, 2012. Your marriage was a true example of real love and marriage the way God intended.

ACKNOWLEDGMENTS

To God be the glory! This book was divinely written by the inspiration of God through the Holy Spirit. God placed the desire on my heart to write a book and create a workbook that would help strengthen marriages and families. Writing this book and creating this workbook has been a long journey, but I know that it was truly by the grace of God that I was able to finish strong. Marriage requires hard work and dedication, and every marriage can be happy and last until death separates you.

I have been blessed with a loving family and would like to thank them for their continual love and support in all of my endeavors. To my parents, Willie and Mary Witherspoon, you are the greatest parents anyone can have. Much love goes out to my siblings Everett, Myrita (Dale), and Shanta. To my nieces and nephews Kyanna, DaQuan, Jordan, Adriana, Adrian Jr. "AJ," Amari, and Elijah you bring so much love and joy to our family. I love you all with all my heart.

A special thank-you goes out to my spiritual mom, El-Brenda Wiley. You cover me daily with your prayers, and I thank you for the love and support that you always provide to me. To my extended family (the Witherspoons and Scotts), thank you for always encouraging and supporting me. To all my dear friends and church family, I cannot thank you enough for your encouragement, prayers, and support.

CONTENTS

1

INSTITUTION OF MARRIAGE

God created marriage and He intended for marriage to last a lifetime or until death separates us. Genesis 1:1 (NLT) says, "In the beginning God created the heavens and the earth." On day six, God created human beings in his own image. When God formed the man from the dust of the ground, He breathed the breath of life into the man's nostrils, and the man became a living person. In Genesis 2:18–22, "Then the Lord God said, 'It is not good for the man to be alone. I will make a helper who is just right for him.' So the Lord God formed from the ground all the wild animals and all the birds of the sky. He brought them to the man to see what he would call them, and the man chose a name for each one. He gave names to all the livestock, all the birds of the sky, and all the wild animals; but still, there was no helper just right for him. So the Lord God caused the man to fall into a deep sleep. While the man slept, the Lord God took out one of the man's ribs and closed up the opening. Then the Lord God made a woman from the rib, and he brought her to the man."

Genesis 24 tells of the story of Isaac and Rebekah. Abraham sent his servant to his homeland to find a wife for his son Isaac. Abraham's servant prayed to God and asked for God's help on picking the right wife for Isaac. Abraham's servant was standing beside a well, and the young women of the town were coming out to draw water. Abraham's servant asked God to show him a sign. The servant said that he would ask the women to give him a drink from their jug and if she said, "Yes, have a drink, and I will give your camels drink also," then he would know that she is the one God had selected as Isaac's wife.

Before the servant finished praying, he saw a young woman named Rebekah coming out with her water jug on her shoulder. The servant ran over to her and said, "Please give me a little drink of water from your jug."

She answered, "Yes, my lord," and gave him a drink. When she had given him a drink, she said, "I'll draw water for your camels too until they have had enough to drink." Therefore, the servant knew that Rebekah was the one God had chosen for Isaac to marry, and as you can see, God truly brought Rebekah unto the man.

Genesis 29 tells of another story about Jacob and Rachel. Jacob met Rachel and Laban, her father, and stayed and worked for Laban for about month when Laban told Jacob that he should not work for him without pay just because they were relatives. Laban told Jacob to tell him how much his wages should be. Laban had two daughters Leah and Rachel. There was no sparkle in Leah's eyes, but Rachel had a beautiful figure and lovely face. Since Jacob was in love with Rachel, he told her father that he would work for him for seven years if he would give Rachel as his wife.

Laban agreed and Jacob worked seven years to pay for Rachel. When the time came for Jacob to marry Rachel, Laban brought Leah to Jacob instead. When Jacob woke up the next morning and realized that it was Leah instead of Rachel, he went to Laban and questioned what he had done. Laban told him that it is not their custom for the younger daughter to get married before the older daughter, but if he worked another seven years for him, then he will give him Rachel too. Jacob agreed and worked another seven years for Laban and eventually married Rachel. How hard are you willing to work for your spouse?

God chose to make woman from man's flesh and bone to illustrate to us how in marriages the man and the woman are joined together, and the two are united into one. It is important to point out how God instructed the man to leave his father and mother and be joined to his wife. The man and woman will now have their own family and should leave their parents out of their marriage. Not only should parents be left out of your marriage but also other family members, friends, and other men or women who are not your husband or wife. You will not be able to cleave to your spouse if you do not leave.

The purpose for marriage is oneness. Husbands and wives should be so unified that they become one. Marriages are important enough to God that He gave us special instructions to help us have and keep a happy successful marriage. Does this mean that your marriage will be perfect? No, it does not. There are no perfect marriages because there are no perfect people.

Our desire should be to not have a stony heart but a heart that is pure. There is no oneness if either spouse has a heart of stone. Love cannot come in and love cannot go out. Ezekiel 36:26 (NLT) says, "And I will give you a new heart, and I will put a new spirit in you. I will take out your stony, stubborn heart and give you a tender, responsive heart."

It takes work to have and keep a happy successful marriage, and one person cannot do it alone. God created us for companionship, and a companion can help us accomplish more than we could achieve on our own. The beauty of companionship is found in Ecclesiastes 4:9–12. The New Living Translation of these verses says that two people are better than one, for they can help each other succeed. If one person falls, the other can reach out and help. A person standing alone can be attacked and defeated, but two can stand back-to-back and conquer. Three are even better, for a triple-braided cord is not easily broken. The three cords represent a husband, a wife, and God. These three form a close relationship that is not easily broken.

In order to have a successful marriage, there are certain qualities that each spouse must have. The first quality is mutual respect: there is no exception for respect in the marriage relationship. The husband must have respect for his wife, and the wife must have respect for her husband. Without mutual respect, there can be continual conflict in the marital relationship. The second quality is mutual concern: the husband should put his wife's needs above his own needs, and likewise, the wife should put her husband's needs above her own needs. When husbands and wives satisfy and meet each other's need, the chances of going outside of the marriage to get your needs met can decrease.

The third quality is mutual sharing: when two people get married, everything they have is to be shared. "What's yours is mine, and what's mine is yours" is how it should be and not "what's yours is mine, and what's mine is mine." The fourth quality is compromising: there is no problem that cannot be solved if the people involved are willing to solve it. In a marriage, the couple must be able to come to an understanding and meet each other halfway. If necessary, agree to disagree without strife.

The fifth quality is mutual love: love is the most important ingredient in any marriage.

First Corinthians 13:4–7 (NLT) says that,

> Love is patient and kind. Love is not jealous or boastful or proud or rude. It does not demand its own way. It is not irritable, and it keeps no record of being wronged. It does not rejoice about injustice but rejoices whenever the truth wins out. Love never gives up, never loses faith, is always hopeful and endures through every circumstance.

The sixth quality is mutual trust: in the marital relationship, each person must learn to trust each other. When a spouse is deceived by another spouse, the deceiving spouse should do all he or she can to rebuild that trust. It is difficult being in a relationship with someone you cannot or do not trust. The seventh quality is total commitment: When two people get married, they are to be totally committed to each other. Let no one split apart what God has joined together (Mark 10:9 NLT). There must be a loving connection and a permanent commitment.

It is important to keep God not only as the head of your lives but also as the head of your marriage. Your marriage must come first, which means that it comes before children, parents, friends, work, hobbies (*before everything* except of course your personal relationship with God). Not only does a marriage require work but it also requires energy. You will get out of it exactly what you put in it. Many couples apply no energy to their relationship but expect their marriage to thrive. If you do not sow into your marriage, you cannot reap anything from your marriage. Therefore, when you start sowing love, you will reap love.

A healthy marriage requires a relationship without fear. You should always be that place of safety for your spouse. Do not belittle or be harsh toward your spouse. First Peter 3:7 (NLT) says, "In the same way, you husbands must give honor to your wives. Treat your wife with understanding as you live together. She may be weaker than you are, but she is your equal partner in God's gift of new life. Treat her as you should so your prayers will not be hindered." Proverbs 31:10–12 (NLT) says, "Who can find a virtuous and capable wife? She is more precious than rubies. Her husband can trust her, and she will greatly enrich his life. She brings him good, not harm, all the days of her life."

Your spouse is a gift from God, and you should guard and protect your marriage as a great treasure. Proverbs 18:22 (NLT) says, "The man who finds a wife finds a treasure, and he receives favor from the Lord." He gets a double blessing (a wife that is a good thing and favor). God brought Eve to Adam, but Adam still had to find her. He gets a wife that God brought to him, and she is a good thing because God made her. You must rejoice in your spouse, delight in their love, cherish them dearly, and not take them for granted.

God expects his children to make marriage a joyful experience. Ecclesiastes 9:9 (NLT) says, "Live happily with the woman you love through all the meaningless days of life that God has given you under the sun. The wife God gives you is your reward for all your earthly toil." Now cherish her and show God that you are grateful for the spouse that he blessed you with. God did not create us to run this race of life alone. Your spouse can help you persevere through difficulty as you do what God has called you to do.

5

In Exodus 17:8–13, we see how the Amalekites came to fight against Israel. Moses instructed Joshua to gather men together and meanwhile Moses, Aaron, and Hur went to the top of a hill nearby. While on top of the hill, Moses held up his staff, and as long as he was holding up the staff, Israel prevailed. However, when Moses let his hand down, the Amalekites prevailed. Aaron and Hur noticed that Moses hands were getting heavy, so they took a stone for him to sit on, and then they got on each side of Moses holding up his hands. As a result, Moses hands remained steady, and the Israelites defeated the Amalekites.

This story shows us just how much we need each other, and more importantly, it reveals to us how much we need God. I'm reminded of another story that I would like to share with you. In Mark 2:1–5 (NLT), when Jesus returned to Capernaum several days later, the news spread quickly that he was back home. Soon, the house where he was staying was so packed with visitors that there was no more room, even outside the door. While he was preaching God's word to them, four men arrived carrying a paralyzed man on a mat. They couldn't bring him to Jesus because of the crowd, so they dug a hole through the roof above his head. Then they lowered the man on his mat, right down in front of Jesus. Seeing their faith, Jesus said to the paralyzed man, "My child, your sins are forgiven."

There may come a time in your marriage when you become weak and need your spouse to carry you and then there may come a time when your spouse may need your encouragement, prayers, and faith. Do you care enough about your spouse to carry them when they are weak? Allow God to use you to be a blessing in your spouse's life as well as those he places in your path. Also allow your spouse and others the opportunity to be a blessing in your life. Do not be so proud or think you have to be so independent that you do not allow others to assist you. A companion is there to help in time of need, and a companion brings comfort and can provide protection in difficult situations.

Our lives are shaped by relationships. Husbands your wife was created by God to help you. Therefore, wives make sure that you learn your husband and know what his dreams, visions, and goals are. Do not tear down his ego, irritate, or criticize him. Instead, help propel your spouse into being the person that God destined them to be. Proverbs 27:17 (NLT) says, "As iron sharpens iron, so a friend sharpens a friend." Therefore, you should marry someone who can challenge you mentally. Two people who bring their ideas together can help each other become sharper.

Accept your spouse for who they are and what they have to bring to your marriage. Do not compare your spouse to someone else's husband/wife. Psalm 139:13–15 (NLT) says, "You made all the delicate, inner parts of my body and knit me together in my mother's womb. Thank you for making me so wonderfully complex! Your workmanship is marvelous—how well I know it. You watched me as I was being formed in utter seclusion, as I was woven together in the dark of the womb."

We all were created to be unique and one of a kind, and there will never be another you. Your spouse has something that you need, and you have something that your spouse needs. Your spouse should not make you feel worthless; instead, your spouse should make you feel like the king or queen that you are. They will bring out the best not the worse in you. If you are not going to help your spouse, please do not do anything to hurt them. Ask yourself, "Am I a blessing, or am I a burden to my spouse?"

Some of the most important things in life involve risk. British writer and theologian C. S. Lewis said,

> There is no safe investment. To love at all is to be vulnerable. Love anything, and your heart will certainly be wrung and possibly be broken. If you want to make sure of keeping it intact, you must give your heart to no one, not even an animal. Wrap it carefully round with hobbies and little luxuries; avoid all entanglements, lock it safe in the casket or coffin of your selfishness. But in that casket-safe, dark, motionless, airless—it will change. It will not be broken; it will become unbreakable, impenetrable, irredeemable. The

alternative to tragedy, or at least to the risk of tragedy is damnation. The only place outside Heaven where you can be perfectly safe from all the dangers and perturbations of love is hell.

What a powerful statement.

Now you can see that love requires you to take a risk. Yes, there may be some bumps and bruises along the way, but love will never give up because love never fails. Can your love withstand a fall? Well, you are not able to have a relationship if your relationship is not able to withstand a fall. Love is a commitment to another person. It is one thing to start something, but the real question is, can you finish it. Any two people can get married, but are you committed to seeing that marriage through until death separates you. You must have a strong desire to want to make your marriage work. Is there anything you can do now to make your marriage better?

The best foundation for marriage comes from the one who instituted marriage. When God is the foundation, you cannot break the covenant. Be committed to God and be committed to each other. God stresses the importance of faithfulness in marriage and how it should be exclusive. Proverbs 5:15 (NLT) says, "Drink water from your own well—share your love only with your wife." In other words, enjoy the spouse God has given you. Proverbs 5:16–17 says, "Why spill the water of your springs in the streets, having sex with just anyone? You should reserve it for yourselves. Never share it with strangers." Therefore, do not do anything to endanger the health and security of your marriage and family.

God wants to protect our marriages, so He is constantly watching us. Proverbs 5:21 (NLT) says, "For the Lord sees clearly what a man does, examining every path he takes." Therefore, please God by showing loyalty to your spouse. True love is seen in what we do. If you genuinely love your spouse, then you will do what is right by them. As a matter of fact, you should always do the right thing especially when nobody is looking (or rather when you think nobody is looking).

Matthew 25:14–30 talks about the things that God entrusts us with. God entrusts you to be faithful and do right by your spouse. Romans 14:12 (NLT) says, "Yes, each of us will give a personal account to God." You cannot focus on what your spouse has done to you or is even doing to you. Instead, focus on what you are doing to your spouse. God is going to ask you about the spouse He entrusted you with. What will your response be when God asks, "Did you do right by the spouse I entrusted you with?"

Every time you think about your spouse, you should thank God for blessing you with your spouse. It is truly a blessing to be married and in love. When you love your spouse, you will want them to be happy. You will want to fulfill your spouse's desires. You will make sacrifices to ensure their happiness. You can demonstrate sacrificial love to your spouse by listening, helping, encouraging, and giving. If you are not sacrificing or giving, then you are not loving. In what ways can you show sacrificial love to your spouse?

Ephesians 5:21–22 (NLT) says, "And further, submit to one another out of reverence for Christ. For wives, this means submit to your husbands as to the Lord." Ephesians 5:25 (NLT) says, "For husband, this means love your wives, just as Christ loved the church. He gave up his life for her." You may not necessarily have to die for your spouse; however, you should be willing to sacrifice everything for her. You will make sure her well-being is a top priority. Wives, you should also make sure your husbands' well-being is a top priority. Husbands and wives, you should be loving each other and taking excellent care of one another. How much time are you investing into your spouse and your marriage?

Do not wait for your spouse to ask you to spend time with them. You should take the initiative and look for ways to serve your spouse. Love your spouse by listening to them. There is a big difference between hearing and listening. You can hear something without really listening. You can be so focused on the words that are being spoken that you ignore the emotions. When you listen with empathy, you are listening without interrupting. You are listening for fears and feelings. Many times your spouse just needs you to truly listen to them. Your body language and facial expression reveals a lot without saying much. It reveals to the other person whether you are truly focused, paying attention, being genuinely compassionate and actively listening. How can you show your spouse that you are actively listening to them?

When you love your spouse, you will value them, honor them, and be honest with them. Every relationship will have highs and lows. Feelings go up and feelings go down. If you want to have a marriage that last until death separates you, it cannot be based upon how you feel on one particular day. John 13:34 (NLT) says, "So now I am giving you a new commandment: Love each other. Just as I have loved you, you should love each other." When you are able to look beyond each other's faults, you will be able to extend love to each other, even during emotional moments in your marriage. Remember, mutual love is a key ingredient to a happy healthy marriage that last until death separates you.

2

YIELD NOT TO TEMPTATION

As the earth populated, so did sin. By Genesis, chapter 4, we are starting to see bigamy, polygamy, concubines, and men putting away their wives for no reason, taking away from God's intention of marriage. Today, we are not seeing much difference. Divorce rates are high, and many families are falling apart. Satan wants to see marriages broken and families destroyed, but God wants to heal broken marriages and save families. God wants to see marriages the way He intended.

Temptation will come, but the problem is not being tempted; the issue arises when you yield to the temptation. Therefore, the key is to not yield to temptation. In Genesis 39, we see how Joseph was tempted by Potiphar's wife to sleep with her, but he refused to give into that temptation. You must be strong and like Joseph run from tempting situations. Second Timothy 2:22 (NLT) says, "Run from anything that stimulates youthful lusts. Instead, pursue righteous living, faithfulness, love, and peace. Enjoy the companionship of those who call on the Lord with pure hearts."

Most importantly, you should not put yourself in tempting situations. First Corinthians 10:13 (NLT) says, "The temptations in your life are no different from what others experience. And God is faithful. He will not allow the temptation to be more than you can stand. When you are tempted, he will show you a way out so that you can endure." When God provides an exit, take it. Many people think that they are stronger than what they really are until they find themselves weak and yielding to temptation. Husbands and wives should be praying for each other daily and seek God's help not to give into temptation. First John 2:15–16 (King James Version [KJV]) says, "Love not the world, neither the things that are in the world. If any man love the world, the love of the Father is not in him. For all that is in the world, the lust of the flesh, and the lust of the eyes, and the pride of life, is not of the Father, but is of the world."

When you focus on satisfying physical desires that is the lust of the flesh. When you desire everything, you see that is the lust of the eye. When you are preoccupied with looking so important, that is the pride of life. Instead of yielding to lust of the flesh, the lust of the eye and the pride of life demonstrate self-control, a spirit of generosity and humility.

I have heard individuals say that they have fallen out of love with their spouse and no longer feel connected to their husband or wife. Many couples live in the same house, but it is like they are roommates and not husband and wife. Can I tell you something? God can renew your marriage and help put that fire back into your marriage. Some people think that the grass would be greener on the other side. They think that they will just find another person who will make them happy and fill their every need. I understand that your spouse may have their flaws and imperfections and so will that other person. It may not be the flaws or imperfections that your spouse has; it may be a totally different set of flaws and imperfections that may drive you even crazier.

Find ways to stay connected to your spouse emotionally and physically. If it feels as if you are falling out of love with your spouse, it could be because you are no longer doing or saying the things you did in the beginning to honor or respect your spouse. Find ways to reconnect with your spouse. Have a passion to satisfy and please your spouse. Think about what it was that made you fall in love with your spouse and why you got married.

What were those things that you did in the beginning of your relationship to sweep your spouse off their feet? Just because you have now accomplished that goal and made that person your husband or wife, you must continue doing those things and even more to keep them. Be creative and seek God's help on ways to spice things up in your marriage. Do not get complacent and let yourself go. You should always want to look good for your spouse. Do not just assume that your spouse knows what you want or need. Your spouse cannot read your mind.

Express your love daily and compliment your spouse. Tell your spouse every day that you love them. Not only should you tell your spouse that you love them, but you should also show them. It does not matter if you were married for one, five, twenty, or fifty-plus years. Let you spouse know that you love them and need them. Husbands, tell your wife that she is beautiful and that you love her. Wives, tell your husband that you are proud of him and appreciate all that he does for your family. Trust me, if you do not compliment your spouse, somebody else will.

Life is too short, and we do not know the day or the hour when our time will come to leave this earth. Therefore, do not allow another day to go by without showing affection toward your spouse. Communication is one of the key ingredients in maintaining a successful marriage. Communicate effectively with your spouse and find out how you can satisfy and meet each other's need. Open up your heart to your spouse and share with your spouse what is going on in your life. Your spouse wants nothing more than to feel as if they are truly a part of your life.

First Corinthians 7:3–5 (NLT) says, "The husband should fulfill his wife's sexual needs and the wife should fulfill her husband's needs. The wife gives authority over her body to her husband, and the husband gives authority over his body to his wife. Do not deprive each other of sexual relations, unless you both agree to refrain from sexual intimacy for a limited time so you can give yourselves more completely to prayer. Afterward, you should come together again so Satan won't be able to tempt you because of your lack of self-control." Please reread this again because God put this in the Bible for a reason.

When we get married, our body belongs to our spouse. Do not use your body as a way to punish your spouse. Marriage requires the rendering of selfish desires to come together for the greater good. In a marriage you must deny I for us. It can no longer be all about you. It cannot be a self-centered marriage but must be a sacrificial marriage that requires servanthood. Serve your spouse with gladness and not with attitude.

Husbands and wives, have fun having sex in your marriage. Keep the passion and find ways to stay connected with each other in the bedroom and outside the bedroom. Just make sure you always feed your spouse (fulfill their needs). Please do not allow your spouse to leave the home hungry (unsatisfied). Therefore, if you have fed them and satisfied their needs, they will not be tempted to stop somewhere else to get something to eat (step outside of your marriage).

God knew that Satan would use sex as a way to try to destroy marriages, and I must tell you that issues with sex is one of the top problems that occur in many marriages today. Men are said to be more physical while women are more emotional. A husband does not want his wife to seem disinterested when they are being intimate with each other just as much as a wife does not want her husband to rush their intimate time together. Therefore, wives, enjoy being intimate with your husband and husbands enjoy being affectionate with your wife. One way to help with this issue would be to communicate your needs, wants, and desires with your spouse. Experiment and explore new ways to satisfy each other.

No matter what is going on in your marital relationship, please do not find comfort in another man or woman. A lot of times, men and women start off just communicating with a person of the opposite sex because they no longer feel that they can communicate with their own husband or wife. When you start sharing your marital problems with a person of the opposite sex, you are inviting more trouble into your life. Please believe that temptation is real. I would suggest that you not play with fire, or you may get burn.

Confiding in a person of the opposite sex who is not your spouse about your marital problems only gave that person the upper hand on what not to do. You already told them all the things that frustrated you about your spouse, so now they know not to do those things and will try to make it look like they can do a better job at taking care of you than your spouse. Do not be fooled by the tricks of the devil and risk losing everything. Think ahead about all the possible consequences that can occur (i.e., contracting a disease or an unplanned pregnancy). I know it is easier said than done, but it is not worth losing your marriage, family, reputation, or career over.

Infidelity is not just limited to physical. Emotional infidelity is increasing in marriages as well. Emotional attachments can and will occur when you least expect it. The more time you spend talking to this person of the opposite sex, the more emotionally attached you can become. The more attached you become, the more time you may want to spend with that person. Since you enjoy talking to this other person so much, you may start looking for an opportunity to spend time together, so you accept an invitation out to dinner or to the movies. All of this is leading up to a physical attachment, and I am certain that there was a physical attraction from the beginning, or you more than likely would not have wasted your time. If you do not stop now, you can fall into an intimate relationship with this person who is not your husband or wife.

I know you think things are all under control. I know you think that what your spouse do not know cannot hurt them. The internet, social media (DMs—direct messages), cell phones (obtaining more than one phone other than business purposes), text messages, FaceTime, sending intimate videos, and dating apps have made it easy to hide what people are doing, what people are saying, and who people are talking to. Remember, you cannot hide anything from God and what is done in the dark will eventually come to the light.

Proverb 5:18–19 (NLT) says, "Let your wife be a fountain of blessing for you. Rejoice in the wife of your youth. She is a loving deer, a graceful doe. Let her breasts satisfy you always. May you always be captivated by her love." Ephesians 5:2 (NLT) says, "Live a life filled with love, following the example of Christ. He loved us and offered himself as a sacrifice for us, a pleasing aroma to God." Our love for our spouse should imitate God's example of His love for us. We should demonstrate a love for our spouse that goes beyond affection to a self-sacrificing love.

Do not ever think that you are too spiritual and will not be attacked by Satan. The devil is sneaky, and he customizes exactly what it is you like. He knows exactly what type of woman or man you are attracted to, and he attacks when you are vulnerable and uncovered. Someone may think that what my husband or wife do not know won't or can't hurt them, but I beg to differ and believe that what is done in the dark has a way of coming to light. Deception makes right look wrong and wrong look right. However, one thing that is for certain is that you cannot hide anything from God. For He sees all and know all.

Here is where the Golden Rule "Do unto others as you would have them do unto you" applies. Whether you are single or married, you are not responsible for the happiness of another man's wife or another woman's husband. If you are single and seeking one day to get married, would you want someone to do to you what you are doing? If you are married, how would you feel if the tables were turned, and the shoes were on the other foot? When tempted to entertain another person who is married or if you are married and tempted to step outside of your marriage, please seek the strength to *just say no*. If you have already entered a relationship with another person who is married, or that is not your wife or husband, it is still not too late to exit. Seek God's strength to break free, ask for His forgiveness, and now receive his mercy and forgiveness.

I hear you asking the question, "Can a marriage survive even after an affair?" Yes, I do believe that marriages can survive even after an affair. I know the Bible says that the only time divorce is permissible is for adultery. However, this does not mean that divorce should automatically occur when a spouse commits adultery. Those who discover that their spouse has been unfaithful should first make every effort to forgive, reconcile, and restore their marriage.

Some people may not stop being unfaithful and this behavior may put the other spouse at risk and only that person can decide on whether they want to stay or leave. Others may try to tell you what they would do if they were you, but once again, remember that you must make that decision on your own. Those same people who said, "If I was you, I would leave" are the same ones who do not leave when they encounter infidelity in their marriage. I am not going to tell you that it is going to be easy. Yes, it will take time to rebuild the trust in your marriage, but if you put forth the effort, in due time, your marriage can be restored.

Can I just point out something? When you forgive a person, you must do exactly that: forgive, let it go, and move forward. If you are still bitter, holding grudges or bringing up the past, then you have not forgiven that person. Forgiveness starts with you. Forgiveness is not for the other person, but it is for you. Make peace in your relationship and show that you are the bigger person. Be willing to compromise and learn how to let some things go.

Satan will try to attack your mind and thoughts, but Romans 12:2 (NLT) says, "Don't copy the behavior and customs of this world, but let God transform you into a new person by changing the way you think. Then you will learn to know God's will for you, which is good and pleasing and perfect." Just because the majority seems to be doing the wrong thing does not mean that you must do the wrong thing as well. It is okay not to follow the crowd and instead seek to live a life that is pleasing to God. Romans 8:5 (NLT) says, "Those who are dominated by the sinful nature think about sinful things, but those who are controlled by the Holy Spirit think about things that please the Spirit." It's only when God renew your mind that transformation begins.

God never intended for marriages to become boring, lifeless, or dull. Real happiness comes when we decide to find pleasure in the spouse God has given us. Many temptations entice husbands and wives to leave when the marriage becomes dull in order to find excitement and pleasure somewhere else. Commit yourself to your spouse and look to each other for lifelong satisfaction and companionship.

God created marriage, and He never makes anything to fail. A marriage joined by God is meant to last. Have a vision for your marriage and understand why God put you together. Your marriage is a part of God's master plan for your life. Psalm 139:16 (NLT) says, "You saw me before I was born. Every day of my life was recorded in your book. Every moment was laid out before a single day had passed."

Be excited about your life and marriage. Pursue your marriage with energy and passion. Matthew 6:21 (NLT) says, "Wherever your treasure is, there the desires of your heart will also be." Wherever you are investing the best of your life, your passion is going to be there as well. The best of your life should go to God, and then the second best of your life should go to your spouse. Are you doing the best in your marriage? Ask the Holy Spirit to teach you how to be a good husband/wife.

The key is not perfection but persistence. After twenty, thirty, forty, and even fifty-plus years of marriage, you should still be very much in love with your spouse. As a matter of fact, the love should be stronger, better, and even deeper from when you first met and got married. Do you rush home to your spouse after work or a meeting because you can't wait to see them and look forward to being in their presence or do you find things to do after work or a meeting to prolong or avoid going home? Well, I hope that you rush home to your spouse and look forward to spending quality time with them regardless of how long you have been married. If not, ask God to give you a stronger desire and deeper love for your spouse.

Being loving and compassionate should not just occur on a special occasion such as Valentine's Day or your spouse's birthday but every day. Tomorrow is not promised to any of us as we can be here today and gone today. If today was the last day that you had with your spouse on this earth, would they leave this world knowing how much you truly love them because you spent every day telling and showing them? Each New Year that God allow you to spend as husband and wife, reflect over the events that took place in your lives together the previous year. Then share your hopes and dreams for your future together. Utilize this time to express your love to each other verbally and/or in writing.

Dr. Gary Chapman wrote a book called *The Five Love Languages*. In this book, he describes five different ways that people give and receive love. Those ways are acts of service, touch, time, giving of gifts, and words of affirmation. Do you know your spouse's love language? If not, I would highly recommend that you discover each other's love language. Remember why you fell in love with your spouse and learn how to show them your affection in their love language. When hard times arise, be quick to forgive and accept forgiveness. You should always look for reasons to restore your marriage rather than look for excuses to leave it.

3

Stand Together

It is so important for couples to be unified as one. Mark 3:25 (KJV) says, "And if a house be divided against itself, that house cannot stand." "Similarly, a family splintered by feuding will fall apart (NLT)." If you do not work together as a couple and stand as one, then issues can creep in and divide you. If you have children, you must be unified on raising your children. Discipline your children together and do not leave all the discipline up to one parent. Make all decisions together whether it is about money or when it comes to rules, boundaries, and disciplining your children.

Children will test their parents and try to play them against each other in order to get what they want. When your child comes to you saying that "Mommy said this" or "Daddy said that," hold your response and check with your spouse to make sure you are on the same page. Do not allow the children to disrespect your spouse. If you see or hear that your child did not listen when your spouse asked them to do something or they talked back to your spouse, immediately step in and let your child know that they will not disrespect your spouse at all. That shows your spouse that you have their back and will always be there to support them. That also shows the children that they cannot come between mom and dad.

Parents, please do not argue or fight in front of the children. It must be noted that whether you argue in front of the children or behind closed doors and the tension lingers on for a while, the children can sense when there is tension between mommy and daddy. This can have many different effects on your children such as fear that mommy or daddy may get a divorce and that their family will be torn apart. They may perform poorly in school or even physically get sick. Parents be that example for your children and allow them to see what a happy successful marriage looks like. Your children should see their parents having frequent date nights, being affectionate with each other, and expressing their love daily. Fathers, your daughters are watching you and will look to date or marry a man like you. Mothers, your sons are watching you and will look to date or marry a woman like you.

Parents, your children will follow your example more than they follow your guidance. They are watching everything you do. They see how you respond to conflict, how you treat your spouse, how you provide and take care of your family. Andrew Carnegie has a quote that says, "As I grow older, I pay less attention to what men say. I just watch what they do."

Most behaviors are established in the home. However, many children or adolescents are not educated or taught at home about God, sex, marriage, drugs, alcohol, and violence. Many adolescents learn about these things from peers, television, or the internet. It is not the responsibility of the school system or church to do all the teaching and educating about these things. The church and school system should be reinforcing and/or enhancing what was already taught at home. The foundation should start at home.

Proverbs 22:6 (KJV) says, "Train up a child in the way he should go: and when he is old, he will not depart from it." Parents train your children and do not let them train you. Disciplining your children does not negate the fact that you are a loving parent. It helps your child/children understand the difference between right and wrong as well as provide direction to their lives. Proverbs 13:24 (NLT) says, "Those who spare the rod of discipline hate their children. Those who love their children care enough to discipline them." Growing up, we were not allowed to be involved in adult conversation. When the adults were in a room talking, the children were in another room

21

playing. A child was supposed to stay in a child's place and stay out of grown folk's business.

It is important that you stand together not only as a couple but also as a family. Joshua 24:15 (KJV) says, "But as for me and my house, we will serve the Lord." Attend church together as a family, pray together, eat together, have daily devotion together, and have fun together. Make sure you are having frequent date nights as a couple and family night with the children.

It is even more important to stand together if you have a blended family. As the nonbiological parent, you should not make demands to your spouse to disown their child and you should not treat their child/children harshly. Instead, make their child/children feel like a part of the family and treat them as if they were your own child. The child was here before you got married, and you still decided to get marry. Therefore, you must accept this reality and make the best out of your situation. Work with your spouse and always support your spouse. Remember that your marriage still comes first (after God, of course).

The Bible provides a clear organizational structure for a marriage. Ephesians 5:21–33 (NLT) says,

> And further, submit to one another out of reverence for Christ. For wives, this means submit to your husbands as to the Lord. For a husband is the head of his wife as Christ is the head of the church. He is the Savior of his body, the church.
>
> As the church submits to Christ, so you wives should submit to your husband in everything. For husbands, this means love your wives, just as Christ loved the church. He gave up his life for her to make her holy and clean, washed by the cleansing of God's word. He did this to present her to himself as a glorious church without spot or wrinkle or any other blemish. Instead, she will be holy and without fault. In the same way,

husbands ought to love their wives as they love their own bodies.

For a man who loves his wife actually shows love for himself. No one hates his own body but feeds and cares for it, just as Christ cares for the church. And we are members of his body. As the Scriptures say, "A man leaves his father and mother and is joined to his wife, and the two are united into one." This is a great mystery, but it is an illustration of the way Christ and the church are one. So again I say, each man must love his wife as he loves himself, and the wife must respect her husband.

Be watchful and alert to people or things that may try to destroy or divide your marriage and/or family. First Peter 5:8 (NLT) says, "Stay alert: watch out for your great enemy, the devil. He prowls around like a roaring lion, looking for someone to devour." Satan does not want to see marriages survive, but God does. James 4:7 (NLT) says, "So humble yourselves before God. Resist the devil, and he will flee from you."

Temptation is real. Immediate actions guard against compromise. Small compromises can lead to devastating defeats. An unrestrained thought, a glance in the wrong place on the internet, a flirting friendship when you are already married each are steps that can take us where we should not go and jeopardize your marriage. When we flee temptation, God will provide a place to run. Allow your spouse the freedom to be honest with you about the issues they may be struggling with. Do not judge them or condemn them and do not get defensive or offensive. Instead, pray for them and ask God to help them through their struggles.

When two committed believers roll up their sleeves and fight the good fight together, they can conquer anything that tries to come their way. The key word here is together. Matthew 18:19–20 (KJV) says. "Again I say unto you, that if two of you shall agree on earth as touching anything that they shall ask, it shall be done for them of my Father which is in heaven. For where two or three are gathered together in my name, there am I in the midst of them." Do not allow the enemy to steal your family.

Be mindful of how you share what is going on in your marriage with others. You and your spouse may have moved on from the issue you were dealing with, but the people you shared that issue with is still holding on to it and holding it against the other person which can make it a little harder for you and your spouse to move forward. Therefore, it is especially important for you and your spouse to work through all issues together and if you need additional help to resolve any conflict then seek help from a professional counselor. Learn how to become one with your spouse and be willing to make compromises. Song of Songs 2:15 (NLT) says, "Catch all the foxes, those little foxes, before they ruin the vineyard of love, for the grapevines are blossoming!" The little foxes are the kind of problems that can destroy a marriage. Do not ignore or make excuses for any issues that arise; rather, identify these problems and deal with them together.

Love really appears when it is tested. Your marriage will encounter some tribulations, but a marriage built on love can stand strong. Marriage requires work, but it is well worth it. Your spouse, your children, and your family are a precious gift from God. Appreciate them, value them, and love them with all your heart. Even though you may hit a bump or come to a crossroad and not know which way to go, keep loving each other until things get better. Be there for each other through the good, bad and the ugly.

In some marriages, couples work against each other versus standing together and working as a team. Andrew Carnegie has a quote that says, "Teamwork is the ability to work together toward a common vision. It is the fuel that allows common people to attain uncommon results." Your spouse is not your enemy or your competitor. You are on the same team, so work together and help each other out. Enhance each other's strengths and cover each other's weaknesses. When one falls, the other helps them up. Support your spouse, take up for them, defend them, and stand with them as they journey through life. Please do not leave them stranded to fight alone. Make sure that whatever you go through in life that you work through it together. Always be there for your spouse, loving them, supporting them, and helping them through whatever life brings their way.

Each spouse will have their own load to carry, burdens to bear, and hardships to endure. What are you doing to help your spouse carry their load, manage their burdens, and endure their hardships? Remember, there is no *I* in team, so in a marriage, you cannot be selfish or self-centered. Real teammates will show consideration for each other's feelings, interest, needs, desires, and preferences. When you do not show consideration for your spouse, then you are being selfish. Do you know that selfishness can ruin a marriage? When two *me*, *my*, or *I*s become one *we*, *us*, or *our*, then you can become closer and stronger as a couple. Couples who are walking in the same direction together, focused on the same things, working together to accomplish a dream or reach a goal will have a greater chance of being successful and accomplishing those dreams.

One person is not doing all the work when you are working together as a team. Couples should develop ways that will allow each person to utilize their gifts, talents, and abilities. One of you may be better at managing the finances. Then that person should manage the finances. Regardless of who is managing the finances, the other person will still know what is going on with the finances and you should work together on your financial goals. If both of you are good at managing the finances, then you can work together to manage the finances.

One of you may be better at cooking. If so, then that person can do the cooking. While the other person washes the dishes. If you both like to cook, then try cooking together or if one person is busy then the other one can cook. The key here is that you are working together as a team. Do household chores together. If you have young children, then one of you take one child while the other person takes the other child to get them washed and ready for bed. Then everyone come together as a family to say your prayers and give good-night hugs and kisses.

Conflict and tension will arise when you are not working together. When one spouse feels as if they are doing everything by themselves, then they will start getting frustrated, bitter, and annoyed. Once these feelings set in, then your relationship can turn cold, distant, and unsatisfying. There is a phrase that says, "United we stand, divided we fall." If you do not work together as a couple and stand together as one, then conflict can enter to divide you and your marriage can fall apart.

Many people were inspired by Barack and Michelle Obama in several ways. The love between Barack and Michelle Obama was not only seen, but it was also felt. Their marriage was admired by many people because it was genuine. They did not have to pretend or put on a show for the public because who they are as individuals and who they are as a couple go hand in hand. Barack and Michelle Obama operated with integrity. They always stood together as one, and they knew how to have fun together and laugh. Does that mean they never had disagreements or always saw eye to eye on everything? No, it does not, because once again, there is no perfect marriage because there are no perfect people.

When couples say, "We have the perfect marriage! We never argue!" The question to ask next, is, why don't you argue or have disagreements? When couples do not have the tools necessary for successful conflict resolution, they tend to believe that any conflict will lead to the end of the relationship. Therefore, couples will avoid touchy subjects or things that may seem too risky to bring up. However, when you are not able to tell your spouse what upsets you, and they genuinely listen to your feelings, then you cannot really get to know each other. You cannot fully experience intimacy in your marriage when you are not able to talk about and accept your differences.

Do you avoid discussing touchy subjects or any feelings that could potentially cause a disagreement with your spouse? Trust me, I totally understand that you do not enjoy being at odds with your spouse. It is never a good feeling. However, you need to see and know your spouse communication and conflict style. You need to know how your spouse deal with conflict, handle, or cope with grief. What makes them angry, sad, or happy? Do they like surprises? Are they spontaneous? Are they a spender or a saver? Do they react off impulse? Do they manage their time well? What kind of work ethics do they have? These are just a few things that couples can argue about. That is why it is so important to take the time to really get to know each other. It is also important to have the skills necessary to deal with conflict in a healthy way, which is necessary for your marriage to thrive.

Dr. John Gottman identified four communication styles that are unhealthy and detrimental to a relationship. He called them the Four Horsemen: Criticism, Contempt, Defensiveness, and Stonewalling. The first horseman is criticism. This is different from a complaint. Criticism is an attack on your partner at the essence of their character. The key here is to learn the difference between expressing a complaint and criticizing.

The second horseman is contempt. When you respond like this, you are being mean. You treat others with disrespect, you are sarcastic, and you ridicule them, call them names, or roll your eyes. The goal of contempt is reached when the other person feels despised and worthless. Contempt is the single greatest indicator that your relationship is in trouble.

The third horseman is defensiveness. This is usually a response to criticism. When one feels unjustly criticized, they then look for excuses, reverse blame to make the other partner feel at fault or play the innocent victim in hopes that their partner will leave them alone. However, the partner now feels as if you are not taking their concerns seriously. A nondefensive response can show acceptance of responsibility, admission of fault, and understanding of your partner's view of things.

The fourth horseman is stonewalling. This is usually a response to contempt. Stonewalling takes place when the listener withdraws from communication, shuts down, and stops responding to their partner. Instead of confronting issues with their partner, people who stonewall will pretend as if they are busy, tune you out, turn away, or engage in distracting or obsessive behaviors. When a person is stonewalling, they may not be at a place mentally or emotionally to discuss things rationally. If you notice that one of you may be stonewalling, then take at least twenty minutes to do something that calms you down such as a walk, run, or listening to music.

Being able to recognize these four unhealthy communication styles and replace them with healthier effective communication patterns are crucial. Your marriage does not have to end when you are faced with challenges with your communication and conflict styles. If you want to stay together until death separates you, then you must learn how to talk to each other when you do not agree. It may look, feel, or even seem as if it is over, however, Matthew 19:26 says, "Jesus looked at them and said, 'With man this is impossible, but with God all things are possible.'" There is nothing too hard for God, and besides, God wants to see every marriage last until death separates you. "Therefore what God has joined together, let no one separate" (Mark 10:9 NIV).

Do not give up on your spouse or the love that you share just because you experience hard times. When the love you have for your spouse is worth fighting for, then when one of you is weak, the other must be strong. When you get angry with each other, please do not allow too much time to go by. You have until midnight to work things out. The more time you spend upset and apart, the more time the enemy have to mess with your mind. You will be so mad at your spouse, and then suddenly someone from your past or a coworker send a direct message to you on social media, call you, text you, come into town and want to see you. Since you are mad with your spouse, you are not thinking clearly, you are in your feelings and you more than likely do not have pleasant thoughts about your spouse.

Now you begin to entertain conversation or more with this other person and enjoying the compliments being given to you. Now you are thinking, "My spouse does not talk to me like this," "My spouse does not compliment me like this," "My spouse does not treat me like this." You start to become intrigued with this person from your past or coworker of the opposite sex. However, please believe that all of this is just a trick of the enemy creeping in trying to destroy your marriage and tear you and your spouse apart. Instead of allowing the hard times to tear you apart, allow the hard times to bring you closer together. Declare right now that no weapon that is formed against you, your marriage or your family shall prosper. The glory of God will rest upon your house.

4

THE VOW

Marriage is a covenant, and a covenant relationship is a sacrificial permanent relationship. On your wedding day, you made several promises to your spouse. First, you made a commitment before God and other witnesses to take each other as husband or wife to have and to hold from that day forward. According to Francine and Byron Pirola, founders and principal authors of *Smart Loving* series, to have is to receive without reservation the total self-gift of the other. It is not a statement of ownership, but rather a promise of unconditional acceptance. Will you have them in spite of all of their qualities (good, bad, and indifferent). Will you have them if they have stains on their credit report? Will you have them if they did not physically look the same from when you first met them? Will you have them if they never had an example of marriage the way God intended?

To hold, according to Francine and Byron Pirola, is a pledge of physical affection and tenderness, a vow to be available to the other in body and soul, a promise to cherish, value and protect the other as we would a prized treasure. Song of Songs 2:16 (NLT) says, "My lover is mine, and I am his." Can you trust them with your deepest, darkest secrets? Can you trust them to embrace your trauma? Can you trust them to kiss your fears? Are you going to be a person of your word and hold onto your spouse in season and out of season? Are you going to be able to accept them being open and honest with you, especially when they speak the truth to you in love?

After you have committed to have and to hold from that forward, you then promised that you would stay committed to your marriage for better or for worse. In other words, you were saying that you would stand together in good times and bad times. We cannot predict what things may come our way, but regardless of what better or worse will look like in your marriage, you cannot allow it to destroy your marriage. Many times when marriages face hard times, they stop having and they stop holding. They put terms and conditions on their tolerance of the other person as well as limits on their companionship. Take the limits off and love your spouse unconditionally.

Another vow that you made was to stay committed to your marriage for richer or for poorer. Whether your finances are plentiful, or you are struggling to make ends meet, you should stand together and support each other. Then you also promised that you would stay committed to your marriage in sickness and in health. If your spouse were to have an unexpected accident or developed a chronic illness, you vowed to take care of them and be there to provide whatever they stand in need of. I have heard of couples divorcing or wishing they were no longer married when one spouse became disabled or terminally ill because they could not handle the other spouse being sick and/or requiring so much care. However, when you said "I do," you were saying that you would love your spouse whether they were healthy or experiencing a health challenge.

Many couples face challenges with infertility and/or sexual dysfunction. Worldwide about 48.5 million couples experience infertility. According to the Cleveland Clinic, some 43 percent of women and 31 percent of men report some degree of sexual dysfunction. While research show that sexual dysfunction is common, many people do not like talking about. I strongly encourage that you share your concerns with your spouse and even to your healthcare provider because treatment options are available. I have an even greater suggestion; turn over your concerns to God. For there is nothing too hard for God. In Genesis 21, we read how God allowed Abraham at the age of one hundred and Sarah at the age of ninety to give birth to a child. God can restore your youth and allow you to still find pleasure with your spouse.

The final vow that you made was to love and to cherish each other from this day forward until death do you part. To cherish your spouse is to respect and admire them above all others. In other words, you must be willing to forsake all others. Be certain to take necessary precautions to protect yourself and your marriage against old and/ or new relationships with people of the opposite sex. First Peter 4:8 (NLT) says, "Most important of all, continue to show deep love for each other, for love covers a multitude of sins." This verse reminds us of the true power of love. Be committed to love, honor, and cherish your spouse always. Remember when you said "I do," you were saying that you were going to always be faithful and devoted to your spouse.

Marriage should be taken very seriously and therefore not entered lightly. A wedding is one day in a couple's life, but the marriage is all the rest of those days that come after it. Do not spend so much time planning for the wedding that you forget to prepare for the marriage. Commitment is a belief that will allow you and your spouse to navigate through the calm and the storms of your marriage relationship. Therefore, for the well-being of your marriage, you must stand together and overcome those situations that would threaten your marital relationship.

Deuteronomy 24:5 (NLT) says, "A newly married man must not be drafted into the army or be given any other official responsibilities. He must be free to spend one year at home, bringing happiness to the wife he married." This scripture shows us how important it is for newly married couples to spend quality time together alone during their first year of marriage so their relationship would have a chance to mature and strengthen. Therefore, protect your marriage from outside distractions. Family and friends of newly married couples should respect their loved one's marriage and not place demands on them that will take away their time and energy from their marriage.

A marriage is like a house in that it must be built. Before a building is built, the foundation must be laid. If the foundation is not there, then the entire building will collapse. Your marriage must have a solid foundation in order to remain standing. As the foundation is built and you continue to build the relationship, the relationship continues to grow deeper and deeper. Just as the roots of an oak tree grow deeper, the roots of your relationship must grow deep. The deeper it goes, the stronger it gets.

Couples must always put forth their best efforts. Once a marriage is built, it must be maintained. Couples must continue to work on their marriage and keep it alive. Couples must continue to make time for each other alone. Couples should not get so complacent that they no longer attempt to keep themselves up. Complacency can dull the sharp edge of love and a lack of passion or energy can lead to unfaithfulness.

Couples should find marriage retreats to attend annually to enrich their relationship. There may come a time when relationships may have a moment where there is a break down. Therefore, occasional repairs to the marriage will be needed. When this happens, the couple must be willing to do whatever it takes to fix the problem. Do not be too proud to seek help from a professional when issues become too complicated in your marriage. Since it is God's will for every marriage to succeed, you should utilize the help and resources that He has provided to get your marriage back on track. Revisit your vows every once in a while to ensure that you are living out those vows and honoring your commitment to your spouse.

Matthew 7:24–27 (NLT) says,

> Anyone who listens to my teaching and follows it is wise, like a person who builds a house on solid rock. Though the rain comes in torrents and the floodwaters rise and the winds beat against that house, it won't collapse because it is built on bedrock. But anyone who hears my teaching and doesn't obey it is foolish, like a person who builds a house on sand. When the rains and floods come and the winds beat against that house, it will collapse with a mighty crash.

Is your marriage grounded? Can your marriage stand against the storms of life?

Someone may be wondering if they married the right person. Just because issues come up in your marriage, you should not start thinking that you married the wrong person. Once you got married, your spouse became the right person. Besides, why did you get married in the first place? We should enter marriage with the right intentions and right knowledge about marriage. When you placed those rings on each other's fingers, you were committing yourself to that person until death separated you.

Many people are driven toward marriage without understanding all they are committing themselves to for the rest of their lives. Marriage is what comes from a commitment to the vow. You must honor your vows for divorce to never be an option. A successful and lifelong marriage comes from living the commitment to the vow. It is all in the vow, and both individuals must be fully committed before they get married. Remember to keep God first in your lives and in your marriage. Ask God to help you honor your vows and have a happy, successful marriage.

Many couples make a genuine commitment at the altar, but their commitment is not lived out in action. Commitment involves action. You must always fight to keep your commitment to marriage first in your lives and resist the pressure to share that commitment with other aspects of life. Few things in this life will remain the same. Things change. People change. Relationships change, and therefore, we need to expect changes in our marriages. Unrealistic expectations are toxic to a marriage. Therefore, do not look for a person or your marriage to be perfect.

Accept the changes that your spouse may go through. Remember that as you mature and grow as individuals, your marriage should adjust and adapt to those changes. Can you humble yourself enough to go through those changes together? James 1:2–3 (NLT) says, "When troubles come your way, consider it an opportunity for great joy. For you know that when your faith is tested, your endurance has a chance to grow." Don't ever deny the pain or hurt that you may have to go through, but always ask what can I learn from it and how can it be used for God's glory? Your marriage is on display for others to see. Sometimes you may go through something in your marriage so that you can be a blessing and help another couple.

Dr. Gary Chapman has a book entitled *The 4 Seasons of Marriage: Secrets to a Lasting Marriage.* In this book, he describes how every relationship goes through four life-changing seasons: summer, fall, winter, and spring. Just like our weather, in marriage, things are hot during the summer season. You are madly in love with your spouse, everything is perfect, they can do no wrong and all you see is the good. During the fall season of a marriage, the honeymoon phase is starting to dwindle. Couples now start to see flaws in their spouse that may have been noticed but overlooked because you were so in love. You may start having some resentment toward your spouse because you are not resolving conflicts well. In the fall season of marriage, couples tend to feel uncertain or less hopeful about where their marriage is headed. The winter season of marriages are characterized by coldness, harshness, and bitterness. When couples go through winter season, they do not feel in love anymore. When couples go through spring season, they start falling back in love.

Ephesians 5:2 (NLT) says, "Live a life filled with love, following the example of Christ. He loved us and offered himself as a sacrifice for us, a pleasing aroma to God." In marriage, you must always walk in love. Strive to see the best in your spouse instead of the worst. We do not deserve God's grace and mercy; however, He consistently gives it to us. First Thessalonians 5:11 says to encourage each other and build each other up. Are you encouraging and building your spouse up?

Love makes allowances for other's weaknesses. We are quick to condemn others for their failures, yet we make excuses for our own. God's love for us has no limitations. Therefore, we must love our spouse without limits. When you said "I do," you were saying, "I am going to take my spouse just as they are flaws and all." When we demonstrate real love, we are setting an example and leaving a legacy of love behind for generations to follow.

Sometimes married couples put on a show in public to make others think that all is well in their marriage; however, when they are behind closed doors, the mask comes off and they are totally miserable. Do you or your spouse have to put on a phony smile around others or can others see the genuine love between you? If you already know that divorce is not an option, would you rather not be happily married versus married and miserable. Do not just endure your marriage because you do not plan on going anywhere. Instead, make the best out of your marriage and enjoy every moment that you are blessed to share with your spouse. It is not merely enough to say "I love you" or promise to do something. Be a man or woman of your word and show your spouse that you love them.

In order to have good relationships, we must demonstrate patience. Husbands, you must be patient with your wife, and wives, you must be patient with your husband. Focus on the good in your spouse and praise them for what they are doing right. Your spouse is still a work in progress, so as those qualities, flaws, and weaknesses that you did not see in the beginning start to come out, do not be so quick to abandon the marriage. Choose your battles wisely and remember that the strongest person can humble themselves. Stop the nonsense and lay aside your pride. Do not allow your pride to get in the way of a lifetime of happiness.

It is good to agree to disagree and even better to do so with mutual love and respect.

Feed your relationship the nutrition it needs to strive. Remember, the striving does not stop after the wedding. Having a wedding is an experience, but having a marriage is a relationship. Grow in love and always be open with each other. There is a saying that honesty is the best policy. According to *Merriam-Webster Dictionary*, "honesty is the best policy" is used to say that telling the truth is better than lying even when it is hard to do. Therefore, be honest with each other and hold each other to the highest integrity.

Love, fellowship, and friendship are important in a marriage. When you spend quality time with your spouse, the love that you have for them can increase. Take the time to learn and really get to know your spouse. Ask yourself the question, "How well do I know my spouse?" Then examine what are the most important things in your life? What are you spending most of your time and energy on?

None of us know how long we have on earth. Therefore, you should make sure you are enjoying every moment that you have with your spouse.

Gospel singer Jason Nelson has a song entitled "Forever," and lyrics in this song reminds us that just as God is committed to loving us forever, we should be committed to loving our spouse forever. "I'll be committed to you. I'll never leave you. Nothing in this world could make me walk away. No matter what life may bring. I'll be by your side. No matter what you face. You won't be lonely. Forever is a long time. That's how long I'll love you." It is my desire for you to have a fulfilling marriage that lasts forever.

5

GOD'S WILL

God's will is for Christians to marry Christians who have godly characteristics.

Second Corinthians 6:14–16 (NLT) says, "Don't team up with those who are unbelievers. How can righteousness be a partner with wickedness? How can light live with darkness? What harmony can there be between Christ and the devil? How can a believer be a partner with an unbeliever? And what union can there be between God's temple and idols?" As Christians, your life should be centered in Christ. Your belief and values are established upon the word of God while an unbeliever's is not.

Not only should you seek to marry someone who say they are a Christian like you but also be certain that you will make a great team. Do they love God the way you love God? Do they prioritize their relationship with God the way you prioritize your relationship with God? Can you see the fruit of the Holy Spirit at work in their life? Philippians 2:2 (NLT) says, "Then make me truly happy by agreeing wholeheartedly with each other, loving one another, and working together with one mind and purpose." God wants husbands and wives to live together peacefully and in love.

Make sure that you marry someone who is fully committed to going through life with you (the good, the bad, and the ugly of life). No matter what life brings your way your spouse should always be by your side, holding your hand, lifting you up. Proverbs 31:10–12

(NLT) says, "Who can find a virtuous and capable wife? She is more precious than rubies. Her husband can trust her, and she will greatly enrich his life. She brings him good, not harm, all the days of her life." Women you should be a blessing to your husband and not a burden.

Proverb 12:4 (NLT) says, "A worthy wife is a crown for her husband, but a disgraceful woman is like cancer in his bones." Proverb 19:13 (NLT) says, "A quarrelsome wife is as annoying as constant dripping." Women, do not irritate, nag, or criticize your husband. Proverbs is clear that men are to find women who have godly characteristics in their lives. The wise man will look to the Lord to give him an understanding wife. When you seek God first, He will bring you the absolute best person that you could marry.

Genesis 24 tells the story of Isaac and Rebekah. Abraham sent his servant to his homeland to find a wife for his son Isaac. Abraham's servant prayed to God and asked for God's help on picking the right wife for Isaac. Abraham's servant was standing beside a well, and the young women of the town were coming out to draw water. Abraham's servant asked God to show him a sign. The servant said that he would ask the women to give him a drink from their jug and if she said, "Yes, have a drink, and I will give your camels drink also," then he would know that she is the one God had selected as Isaac's wife.

Before the servant finished praying, he saw a young woman named Rebekah coming out with her water jug on her shoulder. The servant ran over to her and said, "Please give me a little drink of water from your jug." She answered, "Yes, my lord," and gave him a drink. When she had given him a drink, she said that she would draw water for his camels too, until they have had enough to drink. The love between Isaac and Rebekah started with a prayer for success in finding a wife for Isaac.

For those who may have married a spouse who is not a believer, 1 Corinthians 7:12–16 (NLT) says,

> If a Christian man has a wife who is not a
> believer and she is willing to continue living with

him, he must not leave her. And if a Christian woman has a husband who is not a believer and he is willing to continue living with her, she must not leave him. The Christian wife brings holiness to her marriage, and the Christian husband brings holiness to his marriage. Otherwise, your children would not be holy, but now they are holy. If the husband or wife who is not a believer insists on leaving, let them go. In such cases the Christian husband or wife is no longer bound to the other, for God has called you to live in peace.

It is God's will that you honor biblical marriage (consenting man-woman union) by resisting political pressure to recognize and legalize other sexual preferences. Hebrew 13:4 (NLT) says, "Give honor to marriage, and remain faithful to one another in marriage." God will surely judge people who are immoral and those who commit adultery. Give witness to the depth of God's love for you by keeping your marriage happy and strong.

Encourage other marriages around you to stay strong. Titus 2:4–7 (NLT) says,

These older women must train the younger women to love their husbands and their children, to live wisely and be pure, to work in their home, to do good, and be submissive to their husbands. Then they will not bring shame on the word of God. In the same way, encourage the young men to live wisely and you yourself must be an example to them by doing good works of every kind. Let everything you do reflect the integrity and seriousness of your teaching.

Teach your children the biblical meaning of marriage and pray early for their own eventual spouses and families.

Women, you must allow your husband to lead as God intended. A man cannot love a woman who tries to control him. Women, you were created to be a help mate; therefore, you should not try to control the man you love and were made to help. Men, you must be the leader in your home, for you will be held accountable for setting the order in your home. The wife will not have a problem following the husband when he loves her as Christ loves the church.

Men, stop seeking to fix your wife, and women, stop trying to change your husband. Instead, pray and ask God to work on you and help you be the best husband or wife for your spouse. Despite what they may or may not be doing to you or for you, and regardless of how they may be treating you, focus on being your best and allow God to work on your spouse. Luke 1:37 (KJV) says, "For with God nothing shall be impossible." God can turn your situation around so let go and let God work it out.

Be willing to compromise and leave the past in the past. Give your spouse the right to have their own opinion and do not try to force your opinion onto your spouse. Do not ever threaten your spouse with divorce as a tactic to get them to do something you want them to do. Decide ahead of time not to lose control and say or do something that can harm or hurt your spouse or even destroy your marriage. Strive to create a marriage consistent of forgiveness, kindness, and compassion.

Proverbs 18:21 (NIV) says, "The tongue has the power of life and death, and those who love it will eat its fruit." One word can be a blessing, and one can be destructive. Words can leave scars, and no matter how much you apologize, the damage has been done. Remember, if you do not have anything good to say, then do not say anything at all. It has been said that it takes ten good experiences to make up for one bad experience. Therefore, you should do all you can to create good memories that will last a lifetime and outweigh any bad experiences. Marriage requires work, but it is well worth it.

Since the creation of the world, God intended for us to share our lives with one another.

Marriage is a partnership, and while on this journey called life together, you should grow and develop not only as individuals but also as a couple. Your spouse may see things in you that you do not see in yourself and you may see things in your spouse that they do not see in themselves. You should want to help your spouse become a better person.

Genesis 2:18 (NLT) says, "Then the Lord God said, 'It is not good for the man to be alone. I will make a helper who is just right for him.'" A helper is always there to assist. Wives, make sure you are helping your husband accomplish his goals. Build him up and do not do anything to tear him down. Make sure your home is such a comfortable place that he cannot wait to get home, and then when he gets there, it is so peaceful that it is difficult for him to leave to go to work in the morning. Husbands, you also have a role to play as well. Treat your wife right, value her, and love her. Both of you should be loving, caring, and taking care of each other.

Some of you reading this may have come to a dry season in your marriage and is wondering if your marriage can survive. Well, let me encourage you. Ezekiel 37:1–10 (NLT) says,

> The Lord took hold of me, and I was carried away by the Spirit of the Lord to a valley filled with bones. He led me all around among the bones that covered the valley floor. They were scattered everywhere across the ground and were completely dried out. Then he asked me, "Son of man, can these bones become living people again?" "O Sovereign Lord," I replied, "you alone know the answer to that." Then he said to me, "Speak a prophetic message to these bones and say,
>
> "Dry bones, listen to the word of the Lord! This is what the Sovereign Lord says: Look! I am going to put breath into you and make you live again! I will put flesh and muscles on you and cover you with skin. I will put breath into you, and you will come to life. Then you will know that I am the Lord."

So I spoke this message, just as he told me. Suddenly as I spoke, there was a rattling noise all across the valley. The bones of each body came together and attached themselves as complete skeletons. Then as I watched, muscles and flesh formed over the bones. Then skin formed to cover their bodies, but they still had no breath in them. Then he said to me, "Speak a prophetic message to the winds, son of man, Speak a prophetic message and say, "This is what the Sovereign Lord says: Come, O breath, from the four winds! Breathe into these dead bodies so they may live again." So I spoke the message as he commanded me, and breath came into their bodies. They all came to life and stood up on their feet—a great army.

Despite how it may look or how it may seem, do not give up on your spouse or your marriage. Remember, there is nothing too hard for God. Instead of giving up on your spouse or your marriage, pray and ask God to restore your marriage. God can make spouses grow so deep in love with each other that it will be far greater than ever before. When you do things the way God intends, then things will come together and work out God's way. God honors those who honor him.

In Genesis 18, God appeared to Abraham along with two other men. One of the men asked Abraham where Sarah his wife was, and Abraham responded that she was in the tent. The man then told Abraham that when he returned in a year, that his wife Sarah will have a son. Abraham and Sarah both were old by this time, and Sarah was long past the age of having children. Sarah was listening to this conversation from the tent and laughed within herself, saying, "How could a worn-out woman like me enjoy such pleasure, especially when my master—my husband is also so old?" The Lord asked Abraham, "Why did Sarah laugh? Why did she say, can an old woman like me have a baby? Is anything too hard for the Lord?"

Waiting on God may seem difficult because things are taking too long and not working out according to our plans. When Sarah doubted God, not only did having a baby at her age seemed impossible, but also when it took ten years for it to come to pass, it did not look as if it was going to happen. Due to this unbelief, Sarah told Abraham to sleep with her maiden Hagar, and Abraham listened, and from this encounter, Hagar got pregnant and had a son named Ismael. However, Ismael was not the promised son, and then after the fact, Sarah gets jealous and forces Abraham to send Hagar and Ismael away. Just like many of us, when things do not come together when we want it or how we want it, we take matters into our own hands. However, when we trust God's timing and His process, all things will work out.

Sometimes when it looks like all hope is gone and seem like there is no chance that your marriage can survive, you laugh (HA!) in disbelief that God can restore your marriage. You laugh (HA!) in disbelief that God can restore your youth and allow you to still find pleasure with your spouse. Stop laughing and trust God's ways, his plans, and his timing. God is bigger than any problem that your marriage will encounter. Now which do you believe is bigger, your challenging marital problems or the God who created everything?

God promised that He would never leave us nor forsake us (Heb. 13:5). He never said that we would not face difficulty, but He did promise that He would carry us through difficulties. Numbers 23:19 (NLT) says, "God is not a man, so he does not lie. He is not human, so he does not change his mind. Has he ever spoken and failed to act? Has he ever promised and not carried it through?"

6

KEEP THE PEACE

Just because you are frustrated in your marriage does not mean that you need a new marriage. Ephesians 4:2–3 (NLT) says, "Always be humble and gentle. Be patient with each other, making allowance for each other's fault because of your love. Make every effort to keep yourself united in the Spirit, binding yourselves together with peace." Love will inspire you to become a patient person. When you choose to be patient, you respond in a positive way to a negative situation.

Do not allow your emotions to rule your life. There may be times in your life when you are not going to want to do certain things as well as times when you are going to want to do certain things that you should not do. Therefore, willpower and self-control must preside over your emotions. If your spouse offends you, do you quickly retaliate, or do you stay under control? It is better to hold your tongue than to say something that you will regret later. James 1:19 (NLT) says, "Understand this, my dear brothers and sisters: You must all be quick to listen, slow to speak, and slow to get angry."

Words can destroy in a minute what the heart built in a year. James 3:6 (NLT) says, "And the tongue is a flame of fire. It is a whole world of wickedness, corrupting your entire body. It can set your whole life on fire, for it is set on fire by hell itself." Once those words have been spoken, they cannot be retracted. Therefore, I strongly encourage you to think before you speak. The enemy comes to kill, steal, and destroy. You have invested too much into your marriage to allow the enemy to destroy it.

Sometimes it is not what you say, but how you say it. Do not make demands to your spouse; instead, make gentle requests. For example, if you are trying to get your spouse to help around the house or help with the children, do not be sarcastic or belittle them. Instead be kind to them and come to them in a loving way. Say something like, "Baby, I just love how we work together in cleaning up and getting the kids washed up so we can have some quality time together." I believe that approach will get you further than making your nasty demands. Love and respect will take a marriage a long way.

When you love someone, you should not do anything to intentionally hurt them. Therefore, if you do something to hurt or disappoint your spouse, do not be too proud to say "I'm sorry" or "Please forgive me." Explain to them that it was never your intention to hurt or disappoint them and that you will do everything you can to make it up to them. Now graciously accept the apology and move forward. Proverbs 17:1 (NLT) says, "Better a dry crust eaten in peace than a house filled with feasting and conflict."

Learn how to pick your battles. It is unhealthy for your marriage to argue over every little difference of opinion you have. Give each other some grace and understanding. Pointing fingers and placing blame will not solve anything. Therefore, instead of pointing fingers at your spouse, take full responsibility for your actions and the role you played. Love reminds you that your marriage is too valuable to allow it to self-destruct. Remember that your love for your spouse is more important than whatever it is that you are arguing about.

Set ground rules about communicating on delicate issues. Midnight is not a good time to discuss issues. Set boundaries and specify no dirty fighting. Boundaries could include never mentioning divorce, not bringing up things from the past, never argue in public or in front of the children. No dirty fighting could include no belittling, shouting, cursing, hitting, stomping off, or giving the silent treatment. Remember, love is not a fight, but it is always worth fighting for.

Philippians 2:4 (NLT) says, "Don't look out only for your own interests, but take an interest in others too." Selfishness and control can divide people, but humility can unite people. When arguments and disagreements occur, you can often diffuse them by giving up your right to be right. Even when you don't believe that you did something wrong. I'm sure you think you are perfect Patty or perfect Paul, but need I remind you that there are no perfect people on this earth. For Romans 3:23 (NLT) says, "For everyone has sinned; we all fall short of God's glorious standard."

It is only by the grace of God that we are still here today. When you trust in God, He will turn things around for you. Psalm 34:14 (NLT) says, "Turn away from evil and do good. Search for peace, and work to maintain it." We should work hard to live in peace with others every day. Take some time to examine yourself and your marriage. Then commit to making the necessary changes to improve your life and your marriage.

Create an atmosphere of peace in your home. Ephesians 4:31–32 (NLT) says, "Get rid of all bitterness, rage, anger, harsh words, and slander, as well as all types of evil behavior. Instead, be kind to each other, tenderhearted, forgiving one another, just as God through Christ has forgiven you." With forgiveness, a marriage can be beautiful and endure the hardships of life.

Husbands and wives, both are responsible for the well-being of their home. The leader/head of the family, which should be the husband, accept the overall responsibility for the family. This means that even when you do not believe that something was your fault, you take some measure of responsibility. Since the beginning of creation with Adam and Eve, we see the initiation of placing the blame on someone else. When God asked Adam in Genesis 3:11 if he had eaten from the tree whose fruit He commanded him not to eat, Adam's response is found in Genesis 3:12: "It was the woman you gave me who gave me the fruit, and I ate it." Adam not only blames the woman for giving him the fruit, but he also blames God for giving him the woman.

In Genesis 3:13, when God asked Eve, "What have you done?" Eve replied, "The serpent deceived me. That's why I ate it." We now see that as Adam blamed Eve, Eve then blames the serpent. In marriages and families, neither spouse nor children should play the blame game. Satan was determined from the very beginning to destroy and divide marriages and families. However, we must rebuke his efforts and strive to have a happy marriage and healthy family.

Despite the disturbing circumstance that we may face, we can still be at peace. In John 14:27 (NLT), Jesus says, "I am leaving you with a gift; peace of mind and heart. And the peace I give is a gift the world cannot give. So don't be troubled or afraid." In the midst of troubles peace can be found in Jesus. Thank God that we can come to him with every care and his peace will guard our mind. Galatians 5:22–23 (NLT) says, "But the Holy Spirit produces this kind of fruit in our lives: love, joy, peace, patience, kindness, goodness, faithfulness, gentleness, and self-control. There is no law against these things!" We are called to work for peace and unity through God's spirit and should put on the garments of gentleness, humility, and patience as we seek God's healing in our relationships.

Words are powerful. In just a few words, we could crush someone's spirit or through words of wisdom and hope nourish and strengthen others. Have your words intentionally or unintentionally hurt your spouse? We are tempted to blow up when angry and let words fly without control. Seek God's help to say the right words with the right tone or perhaps to not speak at all. Make sure your words are good, helpful, gracious, and kind.

Remember when you have mutual respect for your spouse, you will not push each other's button. You will not deliberately do or say something that you know will hurt, irritate, or belittle your spouse. Your home should be a place where you find peace and rest. Your home should be a place where you come together and celebrate, fellowship, and make memories together. You should not have to fight your way into your house or even fight your way out of your house. Being stressed out all the time is not a place of peace. Please do not be so holy or sanctified that you are not able to have joy in your home. Have fun, live life to the fullest, love each other and laugh a lot.

Proverbs 17:22 (NLT) says, "A cheerful heart is good medicine, but a broken spirit saps a person's strength." Laugh with your spouse in the good times and even more in the bad times. Laughter can help break through the tough times. Laugh with each other through all the seasons of life you encounter. How can you create more laughter and fun into your marriage?

In Genesis 13:1–9, Abram took the initiative in settling a dispute. Although Abram was older and had the right to choose first, he gave Lot his nephew first choice. Abram shows us how to take the initiative in resolving conflicts. He shows us how to let others have the first choice, even if that means not getting what we want. He also shows us how to put family peace above personal desires. Ask God to help you work together with your spouse and show you how to humbly take the initiative to resolve any dispute. Do not allow your pride to get in the way of a lifetime of happiness.

Conflict comes when communication is missing. Healthy communication can create intimacy in your marriage. Communication involves talking and listening and compromise is necessary. You should be comfortable going to your spouse when you have an issue. However, make sure you always speak the truth in love. Ephesians 4:15 (NLT) says, "Instead, we will speak the truth in love, growing in every way more and more like Christ, who is the head of his body, the church." What can you do to communicate better with your spouse?

Ephesians 4:29 (NLT) says, "Don't use foul or abusive language. Let everything you say be good and helpful, so that your words will be an encouragement to those who hear them." The words that come out of your mouth will either build up or tear down your spouse. Therefore, every day, you should be mindful of the words that you speak to, over and about your spouse. When everything and other people are coming against your spouse, you should be the one who speaks love, joy, and hope into their life. When your spouse shares something with you or acts a certain way, understand the history, experiences, and difficulties guiding their actions. Seek to understand why they do what they do or say what they say. Doing this will give you more compassion when you find it difficult to understand them.

Sometimes, couples approach problems as if their spouse is the enemy, which makes it harder to solve problems together. Instead, remember that you both are on the same team, working toward a better life together. You should be able to settle disputes peacefully with your spouse. Ask the Holy Spirit to help you when you find yourself struggling to resolve conflicts. We can become better at resolving conflict as the Holy Spirit produces self-control, gentleness, and patience within us. What are you doing to stay at a place of peace in your marriage?

Keeping the peace does not mean that you must like all the same things, think, and feel the same about everything. Some couples may be afraid to disagree because they fear exposing their differences will cause conflict and break the marriage. When couples fall into a pattern of reacting versus responding to each other, they will be so determined to make up that they suppress versus discuss their differences. Refusing to acknowledge and accept your differences will lead to other issues. Therefore, when you accept each other's differences, separate pursuits, thoughts, and feelings you can develop more insight into your mutual relationship, which can open the door to greater mutual respect.

Anger is an emotion we all have experienced at some point. Ephesians 4:26–27 (NIV) says, "'In your anger do not sin.' Do not let the sun go down while you are still angry, and do not give the devil a foothold." In other words, regardless of how angry you are, you have until midnight to get that anger out of your system. It is okay to take some time to deal with your anger. Just let your spouse know that you need some time. Just remember the longer you are angry the more time you have for things to become worse, devious plans to develop, bitterness, and an unforgiving spirit to set in.

Galatians 5:22–23 (NLT) says, "But the Holy Spirit produces this kind of fruit in our lives: love, joy, peace, patience, kindness, goodness, faithfulness, gentleness, and self-control." Anything that contradicts these verses should be eliminated from our life. Remember, we have an enemy who will stop at nothing to divide, separate, or even destroy our marriages. God has a purpose and plan for your marriage so please do not allow anything or anyone to destroy your marriage. You and your spouse may not always see eye to eye on everything, but the unconditional love that you have for each other should remain the same.

Peace is not just the absence of conflict, but it is the presence of God's wholeness that allow us to experience true peace. Philippians 4:7 (NIV) says, "And the peace of God, which transcends all understanding, will guard your hearts and your minds in Christ Jesus." God is restoring back to your marriage, that which was eating away at your marriage.

7

UNBREAKABLE

In Genesis 12:1–3 (NLT), the Lord had said to Abram,

> Leave your native country, your relatives, and your father's family, and go to the land that I will show you. I will make you into a great nation. I will bless you and make you famous, and you will be a blessing to others. I will bless those who bless you and curse those who treat you with contempt. All the families on earth will be blessed through you.

When Abram (later changed to Abraham) took on God's name, it meant that they were in covenant. When a woman takes on a man's last name, it means that they are in covenant.

Wedding rings are a symbol of the covenant between a husband and wife. It shows everyone that you are off the market and already taken. You cannot be married and single at the same time. Therefore, if you are not ready for this lifelong commitment, then please think twice before you make those vows. God intended for a marriage covenant between a man and a woman to be unbreakable. In most contracts, there is an escape clause if one person does not live up to his or her part of the bargain, the second person can get out of the contract. However, in marriage there is no escape clause. Some people enter marriage opened to the idea that if it does not work then there is always a way out. However, marriage is not an experiment that you can just test and see if it will work for you.

God created marriages, and He intended for marriages to last until death separates you. Therefore, when God is the foundation of your marriage, you cannot break that covenant. Mark 10:9 (NIV) says, "Therefore what God has joined together, let no one separate." No marriage will be exempt from hard times, but when you have a marriage the way God intended you will not crumble when those hard times come. James 1:2 (NLT) says, "Dear brothers and sisters, when troubles come your way, consider it an opportunity for great joy." Please note that in this verse it said when and not if. When your love is tested (which it will) and hard times come (which they will), keep persevering and do not give up on your spouse or your marriage.

Too many people are impatient with their marriage. If they do not see immediate results, then they give up and do not wait on God to make things better. Isaiah 40:31 (KJV) says, "But they that wait upon the Lord shall renew their strength; they shall mount up with wings as eagles; they shall run, and not be weary; and they shall walk, and not faint." Your spouse is worth fighting for. Your marriage is worth fighting for. Your family is worth fighting for.

When you got married, you were promising your spouse that you would not leave them or forsake them. This meant that you would not physically walk away from your marriage or emotionally detach yourself from your marriage. You can emotionally detach yourself from someone that you come home to every day, but it cannot get better if you emotionally withdraw from it. Being married and miserable is not a good way to be. Therefore, you should do all you can to be all the way in (emotionally and physically).

Family, friends, or other people outside of your marriage may have an opinion on how you should do things, but it is just that, their opinion. The best advice you should adhere to is the word of God. Some people do not want to see you happy and in love or have a successful marriage. They may even become jealous or envious of your relationship. The moment the enemy try to attack your marriage, those same people will gloat and make comments like "I knew they were not as perfect as they were trying to make it seem." Well, that is far from the truth because every marriage will be tested. We are all flawed and will make mistakes. Remember there is no perfect marriage because there are no perfect people.

Marriage is a partnership, and you should be your spouse's strength when they are weak. Lift them up when they are torn down by others. Cover them daily, pray for them, and speak life over them. Even when your marriage is faced with challenges, love each other and work together to make things better. Do not allow stubbornness or pride to get the best of you. Someone needs to be the bigger person and refuse to allow the enemy to come in. Is your marriage Satan-proof?

It takes discipline and self-control in order to have a successful marriage. You must always keep in mind the importance of your marriage. Love your spouse every day as if it were the last chance you get to show them how much they mean to you. Listen to your spouse more, talk less, hold each other more, and argue less. If you have a new day to get things right, then make the decision to let things go and move forward together. You may not understand why certain circumstances or situations occur, but do not get stuck on things you cannot change and stop trying to figure everything out. When moments like this occur, remember the Serenity Prayer: "God, grant me the serenity to accept the things I cannot change, courage to change the things I can, and the wisdom to know the difference."

It is up to you to develop and build a healthy marriage and leave a legacy of love for other couples, your children, grandchildren, and generations to follow. For a strong healthy marriage creates a strong, healthy family. The world needs to see real love displayed through your marriage. Hold tight to your spouse because the tighter the hold, the stronger the bond. Always make sure that you cuddle with each other, hold hands, kiss, make love, have fun, smile, and laugh.

Ask your spouse if they feel as if they are a priority in your life. Do not get defensive to their response; rather, seek ways to change and do better. Now ask yourself how can I make sure that my spouse and my marriage is the top priority it should be? Does your order of importance look like this: God, spouse, children, extended family, careers, and then everything else? If it does not, then you have some work to do to make sure your marriage mimics this.

You must be intentional about building a solid foundation for your marriage. Fire bricks are one of the longest lasting and strongest building materials. Your marriage should be so strong that it is unbreakable and able to stand against the attacks of the enemy. Are you willing to go through the fire for your spouse, for your marriage, and for your family? Nobody is saying that marriage will be easy, but it should always be worth fighting for. It should be evident that you want to walk the rest of your life with your spouse for better or worse, in sickness and in health, until death separates you.

Can you handle the part of your spouse that struggles with trust, insecurities, is emotional, or has anger issues? When you said "I do," you were saying "I accept all of you just as you are, and I accept you for all that is to come" (those things you have not yet seen or learned about your spouse). Can you say that you love your spouse for who they are now as well as for what may be revealed about them later? People may not show you who they really are in the beginning, so ask God to reveal their heart. You can only pretend for but so long. Therefore, do not rush into getting married. Allow yourself some time to get to know each other. More importantly, do not ignore any warning signs that this may not be the right person for you.

Some people will wait until after they get married before they really get comfortable and decide to reveal their true selves. They figure, now that you are married, they got you and who they really are can come out because you are not going anywhere. However, that is not how it should be. You should allow the person you are marrying to see the real you before you get married. The intention is to have a marriage that last until death separates you. It will be difficult to have a happy, successful marriage when both of you are not willing to put in the work and genuinely love each other. If you are not going to be nice and treat that person right, then please do not marry them.

Love is never a burden. If the love you have for your spouse is worth having, then it is worth fighting for. When one of you is weak, then the other must be strong. When hard times come, do not give up on your spouse, your marriage, or the love you share. Romans 8:35 (NLT) says, "Can anything ever separate us from Christ's love? Does it mean he no longer loves us if we have trouble or calamity, or are persecuted, or hungry or destitute, or in danger, or threatened with death?" None of these things can separate us from God's love. Therefore, please do not allow anything to separate you from your spouse.

The rain is necessary for some things to grow, and the storms are necessary for you to thrive. Therefore, if you do not build your marriage upon a solid foundation, it will not be able to stand against the storms that will come against your marriage. The R&B group New Edition has a song entitled "Can You Stand the Rain." Some of the words in this song talk about how on a perfect day,

> I know that I can count on you, when that's not possible, tell me, can you weather a storm? I need somebody who will stand by me, through the good times and bad times. Sunny days, everybody loves them, but tell me, can you stand the rain? Storms will come, this we know for sure; but can you stand the rain? I need somebody who will stand by me, when it's tough they won't run, they will always be right there for me.

When things start to get rocky in your marriage are you going to jump ship or ride the waves? You cannot be so quick to throw in the towel, give up on your spouse or your marriage.

8

BREAK THE CYCLE

Many times, we fail to realize that we do not have to follow the negative lifestyles of our parents or grandparents. Just because your parents and/or grandparent's marriage did not work, that does not mean that your marriage cannot work. Just because your parents and/or grandparents were alcoholics, smoked cigarettes/cigars, used drugs, was unfaithful to their spouse, used profanity, or was even violent, does not mean that you have to follow in their footsteps. Do not allow a negative history to predict your future. Break the cycle now and start your own legacy of positive influences and successes. Abel broke the cycle of his parents (Adam and Eve), and you can also break those cycles that are hindering you from being all God created you to be. Abel learned from his parents' mistakes and lived a life that was pleasing to God. You should also seek to learn from past mistakes whether they are your own or from previous generations and strive to do better and be better.

In Genesis 25–37, we can see generational patterns displayed through several generations. Jacob's mother Rebekah had favored him over her son Esau (Jacob's twin brother), which led to conflict between the two brothers. The dysfunction continued when Jacob favored his wife Rachel (Joseph's mother) over his wife Leah, creating discord and heartache. Jacob loved Joseph over his other children and one day gave Joseph a beautiful robe. Joseph's brothers hated him and plotted to murder him. Although they did not murder him, they did sell him into slavery. Displaying favoritism can be crippling in a family. Therefore, it is particularly important to treat everyone without favoritism and to love everyone in our life as our heavenly father loves us.

Often our attraction and attachment to particular people can carry over from our past. Some people are drawn to those who are like their parents in many ways while others draw to people who are opposite from their parents. Without realizing it, we can carry unresolved childhood conflicts, past hurts, disappointments, and pain from previous relationships into our marriages. Do you have any unresolved issues from your past that are still affecting and/or influencing you today? If so, I would strongly encourage you to let go of those past hurts, disappointments, and pain. Do not make your spouse suffer for something that someone else did to you and do not expect that your spouse will be like someone else who may have hurt or betrayed you.

Many times, people take their pain out on the person who loves them because they cannot take it out on the person who hurt them. It has been said that hurt people hurt people. Pretending not to be hurt, disappointed, angry, bitter, or resentful does not bring about healing. You cannot erase past hurts or pain; however, you can become stronger when you own the difficult parts of your life. It is important for you to live in the truth and reality of what you experienced. Healing oftentimes can come from revealing. Reveal your truth and tell your story. God can use your scars to tell your story.

It is healthy for both your body and mind to let go of past hurts and feelings of resentment. Forgiveness is not a sign of weakness, giving in or condoning a behavior. Rather it is a decision to let go of the negative thoughts surrounding a situation for the benefit of your own health and happiness. Forgiveness breaks the chains of bitterness and shackles of self-centeredness. When Christ forgives, He also forgets. Colossians 3:13–14 (NLT) says, "Make allowance for each other's faults and forgive anyone who offends you. Remember, the Lord forgave you, so you must forgive others. Above all, clothe yourselves with love, which binds us all together in perfect harmony."

Nobody is perfect or will have it all together. Unfortunately, as much as we may want to avoid any type of suffering, we cannot avoid pain, disappointment, or sorrow. For these things help make us stronger, better, and wiser. Some people build walls so high to keep safe from being hurt. They try to protect themselves emotionally by allowing no exchange or feelings with others. Love requires taking a risk; therefore, do not be afraid to let your guard down to love. Seek God's help to heal from any hurt, betrayal, pain and/or unhealthy emotions that you may be experiencing. Your tragedy will either make you bitter or better.

You may have grown up in a hostile environment, your parents may have been abusive, or they had a negative attitude. However, you do not have to be the same way. You can break the negative cycle and create a new legacy of blessings. We may not understand why God allows certain struggles in our life, but we can put our trust in Him even when we do not understand what He is doing. God can use our affliction in unexpected ways. Your past and your pain can be your platform for your purpose.

First Peter 5:7 (NLT) says, "Give all your worries and cares to God, for he cares about you." Your life is in God's hand, and there are some problems that only He can solve. Therefore, you should stop trying to fix things on your own. Trust in God and believe that He will see you through. Jeremiah 17:7 (NLT) says, "But blessed are those who trust in the Lord and have made the Lord their hope and confidence." I encourage you to believe that God can and will work things out in your favor.

Jeremiah 32:17 (NLT) says, "O Sovereign Lord! You made the heavens and earth by your strong hand and powerful arm. Nothing is too hard for you! Your past may have been a mess, but your future can be amazing." Do not allow your past to determine your future. Second Corinthians 5:17 (NLT) says that anyone who belongs to Christ has become a new person. The old life is gone; a new life has begun! Live in your present moment and live for your future, but do not live in the past.

Some people think that because they entered marriage haphazardly that they can get out of that marriage haphazardly. God intended for marriages to flourish and last until death separates you. Divorce is the result of a marriage that God did not put together. Therefore, what God joins together, let no man tear apart. Whenever something is ripped, both sides get damaged. Reconciling may be difficult because you are not certain how the other person will act toward you, love you, treat you, forgive what you did or said. However, when hard times come and your love is tested, keep persevering. Make up your mind today to have and keep a marriage that will last forever.

Each year, reflect over the events that took place in your marriage and share your hopes and dreams for your future together. Love covers a multitude of sins so when you come together as one, the love that you have for each other will overpower everything else. It takes a real man and a real woman to acknowledge that they have not been the husband or wife they needed to be. The kind of father or mother they needed to be. The kind of person they needed to be.

Despite any choices, circumstances, surprises, or shortcomings that may have landed you in a less-than-perfect situation, you should not look for the past to make it better. Instead, you can commit to a better future. Leave the past in the past. God loves us unconditionally and his mercies are new every day. Lamentations 3:22–23 (NLT) says, "The faithful love of the Lord never ends! His mercies never cease. Great is his faithfulness; his mercies begin afresh each morning."

Not only must you forgive those who have hurt you, but you must also forgive yourself. Forgive how you failed, how you messed up, how you caused hurt to someone, or even how you broke your vows. Remember that God still loves you. Second Corinthians 12:9 (NIV) says, "But he said to me 'My grace is sufficient for you, for my power is made perfect in weakness.'" Therefore I will boast all the more gladly about my weakness so that Christ's power may rest on me. When we recognize our limitations, then we can depend more on God for our success rather than leaning on our own strengths or efforts.

There is no bondage that God cannot break you free from. Even damaged hearts can be mended. Gospel singer Jekalyn Carr has a song titled "You're Bigger," and in this song, she reminds us that God is bigger than any problem that we will encounter. God is bigger than any marital problem. God is bigger than any financial problem. God is bigger than our mistake. There is nothing too big or small for God. Which do you think is bigger, your worst problem, or the God who created everything?

Your spouse may get on your nerves at times; your spouse may even do something to hurt your feelings. However, you should be grateful that you have a spouse to get on your nerves. That person who lost their spouse to death can only hope that they still had their spouse around. Therefore, do not let the night go by with you not talking to your spouse or with you being angry with your spouse. Shake it off, keep it moving, and get past whatever is trying to divide you. No matter how upset you may get with your spouse, leaving should not be an option. More importantly, you should not do something so detrimental to your spouse that he or she would even want to leave.

9

FULFILL YOUR
SPOUSE'S DESIRES

Gifts often appreciated the most are not those that are the most expensive, but those that reflect investment of yourself in considering the desires and wants of the other person. You may be surprised, but it is often the little things that you do for spouse that will go a long way to make your spouse feel special and important to you. Are you listening when your spouse shares their inner most wants and desires? If your spouse shares with you that they would love to walk the beach at sunset or see their favorite sports team. Do you have a passion to fulfill those desires or wants?

Ask yourself this question, "Do I treat others better than I treat my spouse?" Well, you should treat your spouse like the king and queen that they are. Women, create a king's day for your man. Sit and talk with your husband about the things that he would like to do in a day. This day would consist of everything *he* likes (it is not about you, ladies, on this day). He gets to dictate how this day would go. You just make it happen.

Men, likewise, you will create a queen's day for your woman. Sit and talk with your wife about the things that she would like to do in a day. This day would consist of everything *she* likes (it is not about you, men, on this day). She gets to dictate how this day would go. You just make it happen.

There is a saying "Anything worth having is worth sacrificing and working for." Is your spouse worth the sacrifice? Are you investing your time, energy, and money on your spouse? Have you taken the time to learn your spouse? Do you know your spouse well enough that you can finish their sentence? Can you tell when your spouse is having a bad day or not feeling well (even if they do not voice it)? Are you able to recognize the times when your spouse really needs your support and provide it (even if they say they don't)?

God created man for relationship. Take time to establish and develop your relationship. Spend time with each other. Communicate with each other openly and honestly. Know each other. Trust each other. Depend on each other. Understand each other and express yourself to each other. This is how one can build a solid foundation and have a marriage that last a lifetime.

Genesis 2:25 (NLT) says, "Now the man and his wife were both naked, but they felt no shame." In a marriage the way God intended, a husband and wife would have no barriers or feel no embarrassment in exposing themselves to each other. However, in marriages, couples create barriers to hide areas they do not want their spouse to know about. In order to have a marriage the way God intended spouses must be able to be naked and not ashamed. Be real about your flaws and imperfections. Do not be afraid that your spouse will not love you or want to be with you if they knew the real you.

Be authentic and be who you are. Love without limits. Do not have a hidden agenda or ulterior motive but love your spouse with a pure heart. Matthew 5:8 (NLT) says, "God blesses those whose hearts are pure, for they will see God." Build pure intimacy and make your marriage a safe haven. Do you consider your spouse's feeling and situation when pursing intimate time together? Do you look forward to these intimate moments with your spouse?

I have heard many couples say how they married their best friend. A friend is someone with whom you feel comfortable. A person whose company you prefer over another's. A person you can count on for support, encouragement, and all-out honesty. A true friend believes in you. When you hurt your friend hurts. Galatians

6:2 (NLT) says, "Share each other's burdens, and in this way obey the law of Christ."

A friend is someone who gives you safety and trust. A friend is a person whom you can be yourself. Which means you can be totally exposed and open. A friend can see you at your worst as well as at your best and still love you just the same. Friends pray for each other and with each other. A true friend is there when you need them the most. Proverbs 18:24 (NLT) says, "There are 'friends' who destroy each other, but a real friend sticks closer than a brother."

Do not just look to find a true friend; rather, seek to become one. You should challenge your spouse to reach their greatest potential. Your spouse should be a better person then when you first got married. Learn from each other and help each other grow mentally, emotionally, and spiritually. You should genuinely want what is best for each other.

If something is important to your spouse, then it should be important to you. Listen carefully to your spouse and take a personal interest in what they enjoy and appreciate. Song of Solomon 5:16 (KJV) says, "His mouth is most sweet: yea, he is altogether lovely. This is my beloved, and this is my friend, O daughters of Jerusalem." In a healthy marriage, lovers should also be good friends. A friendship is nurtured through the good and bad times. Friends share their hearts, but they do not step on each other's heart.

When the love between a husband and wife is real, then one woman would be enough to satisfy that one man and one man would be enough to satisfy that one woman. Your spouse should be all you need. Song of Solomon 7:10 (KJV) says, "I am my beloved, and his desire is toward me." It is only in marriage that the complete union of mind, heart, and body can be recognized. Let your spouse know that if you had to do it all over again, you would want to marry them without a second thought.

Love is a choice, and you grow in love. You do not fall in love because if you fall in love, you can also fall out of love. Your love is the foundation for your marriage. Love makes a marriage beautiful, and love grows out of an attitude of honor. You must always esteem and respect your marriage. Your marriage should be more important than any issues that could arise. Your marriage requires you to care about each other and you should show your spouse affection and give your spouse the attention they deserve.

Despite our flaws and imperfections, God still love us and we too must show this type of love to our spouse. First John 3:16 (NLT) says, "We know what real love is because Jesus gave up his life for us. So we also ought to give up our lives for our brothers and sisters." Real love is an action, and it produces selfless sacrificial giving. A successful marriage requires sacrifice. When you get married, it can no longer be all about you. It is now about putting someone else's needs above your own. You should be willing to serve your spouse with gladness and not with attitude.

Are you your spouse's biggest fan? Do you support their endeavors? Well, you should not be jealous or envious that your spouse is successful. Instead you should want to see your spouse successful in all that they do and be there every step of the way making sure and helping them reach their highest potential. Remember you are not nor should you be in competition with your spouse. Your spouse should enhance your existence.

In order to have a happy, successful marriage, you must be all the way in. You cannot pick or choose to be married on certain days or at certain times. You must be totally committed. Stay committed when things are good and when things are not so good. Learn how to work through challenging moments. There is purpose in our challenges, and without them, we would not reach our full potential. Do not be so quick to give up and throw in the towel.

Pretending that everything is okay will not make everything okay. Address the elephant in the room immediately and stop sweeping everything under the rug. Ignoring a problem or situation only causes it to get bigger and worse. Do not allow another second to go by being at odds with your spouse. Remember, tomorrow is not promised.

Ephesians 4:26–27 (NLT) says, "'Don't sin by letting anger control you.' Don't let the sun go down while you are still angry, for anger gives a foothold to the devil." Stop counting how many times you have to forgive your spouse. You must be able to forgive the unforgiveable and unimaginable. Staying angry only gives the devil an advantage over us. Do you argue to try to prove your point, or do you look to see things from your spouse perspective? Seek to understand your spouse rather than trying to be understood.

Often, when we are convinced that we are right, we do not want to hear what the other person has to say. Have you ever wondered what it is like to be married to you? Instead of looking for God to change your spouse, God is looking to change you and do a work in and through you. God alone can meet our deepest needs and give us soul deep satisfaction.

Psalm 37:3–4 says, "Trust in the Lord and do good. Then you will live safely in the land and prosper. Take delight in the Lord, and he will give you your heart's desires." When you pay attention to your spouse's preferences or needs, they can know and trust that you are able to decide or choose things that they will like without them being there. Do not struggle with trying to figure out your spouse's desires. Instead of guessing what your spouse wants, simply just ask them, "Honey/baby what do you want?" That simple way of communicating can alleviate unnecessary stress.

10

A Ruth and Boaz
Kind of Love

The book of Ruth demonstrates how Ruth and Boaz developed an unselfish love and deep respect for each other. Ruth's first husband Mahlon died as well as her father-in-law and brother-in-law. Ruth decided to go with her mother-in-law Naomi to Bethlehem, which is her mother-in-law's homeland. Ruth went out to gather grain behind the harvesters in Boaz's field in order to obtain food for Naomi and herself. Boaz noticed Ruth and inquired about who she was. Upon finding out her identity, Boaz gave Ruth special privileges of gleaning right behind the young women.

Once Ruth returned home to her mother-in-law, Naomi questioned where Ruth worked, and Ruth told her mother-in-law about the man in whose field she had worked. Naomi explained to Ruth that Boaz was a close relative and one of the family redeemers. During the time period of the text, a family redeemer was a relative who volunteered to take responsibility for the extended family. When a woman's husband died, the law provided that she could marry a brother of her dead husband. However, in this situation Naomi had no more sons. Therefore, the nearest relative of the deceased husband could become a family redeemer and marry the widow.

Naomi gave Ruth specific instructions to follow in accordance with Israelite custom and law. By observing this custom, Ruth would inform Boaz that he could be her family redeemer. Boaz recognized Ruth's loyalty and confirmed that he was indeed one of her family redeemers, but there was another man who was even closely related to her. Boaz informed Ruth that he would talk with the other man, and if the other man was willing to marry her, then he should marry her. However, if the other man was not willing to marry Ruth, then Boaz was more than willing to marry her.

Boaz called ten leaders from the town and asked them to be witnesses as he held a conversation with the other family redeemer. He started the conversation by letting the other relative know that Naomi was back in town and was selling the land that belonged to their relative Elimelech (Naomi's deceased husband). Boaz told him that he could redeem the land if he wished and could buy it now in the presence of the witnesses. However, if he did not want to buy the land then let him know right away because he was next in line to redeem it.

Initially, the man replied that he would buy the land. Then Boaz informed him that if he brought the land, he was also required to marry Ruth. Upon hearing that information, the man changed his mind and stated that he could not redeem it. In the presence of the witnesses, Boaz brought the land and accepted to take Ruth as his wife. Boaz married Ruth, and they became the parents of Obed who was the father of Jesse, the grandfather of David and a part of the lineage of Jesus Christ.

God's purpose and plan for our lives are far greater than the plan that we have in mind for our lives. Isaiah 55:8–9 (NLT) says, "My thoughts are nothing like your thoughts, says the Lord. And my ways are far beyond anything you could imagine. Just as the heavens are higher than the earth, so my ways are higher than your ways and my thoughts higher than your thoughts." Instead of trying to make God's plan and purpose fit into ours we should conform to God's plan for us. Father, not my will, but let your will be done.

Many times in life, we do not end up with our first choices. Sometimes not even our second or third choices. However, one thing that I found out is that our first, second, or even third choice was not God's best choice for us. Do not be saddened by closed doors. Trust that when God closes a door that it is for your good and that he has something better planned for you. God's timing is perfect and will be just what you need when you need it. Revelation 3:8 (NLT) says, "I know all the things you do, and I have opened a door for you that no one can close." One thing I have learned on this journey called life is that nothing happens by happenstance. The right man or woman that God has for you will have the right to redeem you. It will not feel good; it will feel right. It will look right, and all will be right.

Boaz was attracted to Ruth's character and despite his desire to want to marry Ruth, he did not scheme or manipulate anyone or anything in order to be with Ruth. Boaz demonstrated integrity and went about redeeming Ruth the right way. The plan of God was advanced because of Ruth and Boaz's union. When a divine connection happens, more than the people in the relationship get blessed by the union.

Ruth's life displayed good qualities as she was loyal, hardworking, loving, kind, patient, and faithful. She exhibited these qualities consistently in every area of her life. No matter what Ruth did or wherever she went, her character never changed. Boaz was the right redeemer, and he immediately recognized the virtuous woman that Ruth was, and he had a genuine desire and will to marry her. Do you have a genuine desire for your spouse? Do you have an unselfish love and deep respect for your spouse? Relationships and love require a sacrifice and should be well worth the investment.

Be open to love and let love guide you. If you genuinely want to be with the other person, then take ownership of the relationship. Boaz did not hesitate in letting Ruth know that he wanted to marry her. It is time to stop playing games and playing hard to get. If you desire a Ruth and Boaz kind of love, then ask God to change your way of thinking and open your heart and eyes to love. Only God can remove the scales off your eyes and allow you to see the beauty of love standing right in front of you.

Love requires taking a risk. When you genuinely love someone, you do not want to live your life without that person. In Ruth
1:16–17 (NLT),

> Ruth replied to her mother-in-law, "Don't
> ask me to leave you and turn back. Wherever you
> go, I will go; wherever you live, I will live. Your
> people will be my people, and your God will be
> my God. Wherever you die, I will die, and there I
> will be buried. May the Lord punish me severely
> if I allow anything but death to separate us!

Wow! What a powerful statement. Ruth was truly a devoted
woman. According to *Cambridge Academic Content Dictionary*,
devoted is defined as "extremely loving and loyal." Are you this
devoted to your spouse? Love is powerful. Take the time to tell your
spouse how much you love them. There is power in words, and your
spouse needs to know how much they mean to you. As a matter of
fact, why don't you express your love to your spouse in a love letter?
You can even read the letter to them. I am sure that would really
mean the world to them and leave a lasting impression.

Maya Angelou said, "I've learned that people will forget what
you said, people will forget what you did, but people will never forget
how you made them feel." Are you doing all that you can to make
sure that your spouse will never forget how good you made them feel?
More than your words, your actions will have a tremendous impact
on your marriage. First John 3:18 (NLT) says, "Dear children, let's
not merely say that we love each other; let us show the truth by our
actions." Small acts of kindness will last a lifetime.

When you have your spouse back, front, side, and bottom, you
show the world and Satan that together you and your spouse are fully
covered and unstoppable. Ecclesiastes 4:9–12 (NLT) says, "Two people are better off than one, for they can help each other succeed. If
one person falls, the other can reach out and help. But someone who
falls alone is in real trouble. Likewise, two people lying close together
can keep each other warm. But how can one be warm alone? A per-

son standing alone can be attacked and defeated, but two can stand back-to-back and conquer. Three are even better, for a triple-braided cord is not easily broken." You and your spouse are better together, and with God as the head of your marriage, you are a force to be reckoned with.

Some of you reading this may have encountered an experience of what love looks like in action with your spouse. Now several years into your marriage, your spouse will not take you to the doctor, pick up or set up your medications, fix you something to eat, or a give you a glass of water. Now you are pondering what changed. How did we get here?

May I remind you that when you got married, you vowed to love your spouse in sickness and in health, for richer and for poorer, for better and for worse. Now ask yourself these questions. Would I still love my spouse even if they lost their job and could no longer provide the financial support they once did? Would I still love my spouse even if they made the wrong choice or a bad decision? Would I still love my spouse even if they were diagnosed with a terminal illness months after we got married? Would I still love my spouse if they lost their hair that I love so much? Would I still love my spouse even if they were severely burned and did not have that pretty/handsome face that I adore? Would I still love my spouse even if they could no longer walk, talk, or feed themselves? Would I still love my spouse even if they lost their memory and no longer knew who I was?

First John 4:9 (NLT) says, "God showed how much He loved us by sending his one and only son into the world so that we might have eternal life through him." Now that is love! Song of Songs 8:6–7 (NLT) says,

> Place me like a seal over your heart, like a seal on your arm. For love is as strong as death, its jealousy as enduring as the grave. Love flashes like fire, the brightest kind of flame. Many waters cannot quench love, nor can rivers drown it. If a man tried to buy love with all his wealth, his offer would be utterly scorned.

Although death is inevitable, the bond of love is steady, unshakable, and broken only in death. Love cannot be destroyed by time or disaster and cannot be brought for any price because love is freely given. Love must be accepted as a gift from God and then shared within the guidelines that God provides. Accept the love of your spouse as God's gift and strive to make your love a reflection of the perfect love that comes from God himself.

When you love your spouse unconditionally, you never stop loving them. You love *all* of them. *All* that is seen now and even *all* that may come later. Can you handle the part of your spouse that struggles with trust, is insecure, have anger issues, control issues, is emotional, or sensitive? When you said "I do," you were saying I want *all* of you just as you are and for *all* that is to come. Humility is valued over pride and love shows its worth in undeserved mercy and kindness. When you are able to be naked (open) and unashamed (honest) with your spouse and allow them to see the real you and they still love you and want to spend the rest of their life with you… that is love!

Love is about finding that person who brings out the best in you and wants the best for you. First Corinthians 13:4–7 (NIV) shows us the way God wants us to love.

> Love is patient, love is kind. It does not envy, it does not boast, it is not proud. It does not dishonor others, it is not self-seeking, it is not easily angered, it keeps no record of wrongs. Love does not delight in evil but rejoices with the truth. It always protects, always trusts, always hopes, always perseveres.

When the love is real, you will fight for your marriage and always protect your marriage. Do you have a Ruth and Boaz kind of love?

Maya Angelou has a quote that says, "Love recognizes no barriers. It jumps hurdles, leap fences, penetrates walls to arrive at its destination full of hope." Have you ever seen a couple and said, "Look at those lovebirds" or even had someone say to you how you and your spouse are so "lovey-dovey" (very affectionate or romantic)? Well, the actual lovebird is one of the smallest members of the parrot family. As their name suggest, lovebirds are known for the loving, attentive bond they tend to form with their mates. Lovebirds are chatty, sings, and whistle all day. However, lovebirds usually do not talk in the way you would expect them to. Instead, they talk to each other and not so much to people.

Husbands and wives, just like the actual lovebirds, you should always want to talk to each other about any and everything. Tune the world and everyone else around you out so you can bond with each other, focus on your marriage, and remain committed to each other. Remember, on your wedding day you made a vow that "I... take you...to be my wife/husband, to have and to hold from this day forward; for better, for worse, for richer, for poorer, in sickness and in health, to love and to cherish, till death do us part, according to God's holy law. In the presence of God, I make this vow." You made these vows before God, in front of family and friends declaring that you would always love and care for each other in a way that will please God.

Marriage is a covenant, and a covenant is based on mutual commitment. Are you committed to loving your spouse "for better or for worse"? Are you willing to walk the rest of your life with your spouse "in sickness and in health"? Do you love your spouse enough to change their dressing if they have wounds, a colostomy bag, a catheter bag, or wearing adult diapers? We need God to help us honor him and his covenant of marriage. You should not be ready to walk away from your spouse the minute they no longer line up to your expectations, or they no longer make you happy, or someone else comes along.

Ecclesiastes 7:8–9 (NLT) says, "Finishing is better than starting. Patience is better than pride. Control your temper, for anger labels you a fool." Anyone can get married, but do you have what it takes to stay married. Having a happy successful marriage that lasts until death separates you requires hard work, self-discipline, wisdom, and patience. Do not start an argument. If someone else starts an argument, then you should end it. Humble yourself and do not allow pride to divide you and your spouse. Always be patient and kind to each other.

In 2020, we experienced a global pandemic. The United States alone had over 78 million people that were infected with coronavirus (COVID-19). Unfortunately there were over 918,000 deaths in the United States. Globally, there were a total of over 410 million people infected with coronavirus (COVID-19) and around 6 million deaths. Millions of people were left unemployed, and several relief packages were needed to help Americans. Due to an outbreak of the coronavirus, many states had mandatory shutdowns and people had to quarantine at home for weeks, countries were put under lockdown, and restrictions were placed on traveling. Mask mandates were ordered, and there were limitations on how many people could gather at weddings, funerals, graduations, and even family gathering for holidays.

Marriages and families were tested. Couples were forced to spend time together like they never have done before. Being around each other 24–7 drove some couples crazy. While it brought others closer together. Many couples utilized this time of quarantining together as an opportunity to really get to know each other. They learned things about their spouse that they never knew. They communicated with each other more than ever. They were more affectionate with each other, and they became creative and found ways to have fun and spice things up in their marriage.

Prior to the pandemic, the business of life took away these precious moments. However, since the pandemic, many people's eyes have been opened and they realized the importance of not taking life nor one's spouse for granted. The coronavirus pandemic affected every family differently. Some family members contracted the coronavirus and survived while other family members who contracted the coronavirus did not survive. One spouse contracted the coronavirus, and the other spouse did not contract the virus. Both spouses contracted the coronavirus and quarantined together. Some people had mild symptoms, some people had severe symptoms and some people did not have any symptoms.

Ecclesiastes 7:2 reminds us that death is the destiny for every-one. Many people may not feel comfortable talking about death and do not want to think about or deal with death. However, the reality of it is that life is short, and we all only have a certain amount of time to live and love well. Since we do not know in advance the day or the hour that death will come upon us, I encourage each of you reading this book to make the best out of every opportunity you get to live together as husband and wife. Do not postpone those things you want to experience together. An unknown author wrote, "People waste so much time waiting for the 'right time'—tomorrow is never promised. If you feel it, do it."

Do not allow yourself to get so comfortable in your marriage that you become predictable. You go the same places, you have the same routine, you do the same things, you are intimate with your spouse the same way for twenty, thirty, forty, and fifty-plus years. May I suggest something to you? Try new things, go places you have never been before, do things you have never done before, eat foods you have never tried before. Even God do not always do things in our lives the same way He did them before or even how He does them for others. God will not heal us, bless us, deliver us, or even speak to us the same way. Therefore, I encourage you to change things up in your marriage, spice things up and blow your spouse's mind.

11

THE RIGHT MOTIVES

Oftentimes, people do not marry for all the right reasons. Some marry because they were with the other person so long that it seems like the right thing to do. True, you may have a history together; however, you both must have a genuine love for the other. Fear of getting back into the dating world should not be a reason to get marry. I get it, you know what you got, but you do not know what you will get. Well, if you trust God, trust that He will put you in the right place at the right time with the right mate.

Two incomes are better than one, right? However, getting married just for financial gain is not the answer. Sure, he may have a great job, or sure, she may have good credit, but do you really love him or her. If you are selfish and only care about yourself, then putting your spouse's needs and/or desires before yours could be a challenge. It is going to take more than the two of you looking good together and money definitely cannot buy you love.

One thing is for certain. You cannot change anybody. Therefore, whatever bothered you about the other person before you got married; getting married will not change anything. Remember when you get marry, you are accepting the other person just as they are (flawed and all that comes with them). Do not be afraid to walk away if you are not sure that you want to marry the other person. It would be better to let the relationship go before you get married then to wait until after you get married and have to dissolve the marriage.

Getting married due to an unexpected pregnancy or not wanting to have a child out of wedlock is not a reason to get married. I understand that may not have been what you planned for your life, but you were not the first and you will not be the last. Marry because the two of you genuinely want to spend the rest of your life together and have a real unconditional love for each other.

Please do not get married just because you believe your biological clock is ticking. When you allow the fear of being alone or not having children by a certain age be the reason you get married, then you may start looking desperate and settle for just anybody. Wait on God and trust his timing. Sarah was ninety years old when she got pregnant, and Isaac was forty years old when he got married. Therefore, do not allow others to put pressure on you. Get married because you know without a shadow of doubt you are marrying the man or woman that God has for you. Remember, what God has for you is for you and nothing or nobody can stop or block your blessing (other than you).

It is totally understandable. Waiting can be difficult. When things do not happen when we want them to, we start questioning God and his timing. Isaiah 40:31 (KJV) says, "But they that wait upon the LORD shall renew their strength; they shall mount up with wings as eagles; they shall run, and not be weary; and they shall walk, and not faint." Waiting is one of life's best teachers. In waiting, we develop endurance, the ability to trust God's love and goodness even when things are not going our way. I encourage you to wait in hope, knowing that God will come through for you at just the right time.

Proverbs 3:5–6 (NLT) says, "Trust in the Lord with all your heart; do not depend on your own understanding. Seek His will in all you do, and He will show you which path to take." When you seek God, He will bring you the person that you need. The right man or woman that God has for you will do what is right by you. Marry a man or woman who values you and loves you for who you are. Destiny cannot be denied, and destiny is the will of God (it is what God wants).

Be mindful of what you are asking God for. If you are praying for a husband or wife, then you must know why you want a husband or wife. Make sure your motives are pure, and you are not just looking for someone to have on your arm (do not just look for physical attraction). When God blesses you with a husband or wife, you must take care of that husband or wife.

I am sure you are wondering how you will know when you have found the right person. Well, as I have been told several times, "You just know." Upon asking "How do you just know?" The response will be "You just do." There will not be any second-guessing, and you will know without a shadow of doubt. Your connection will be on another level. It will not be like anything you have ever experienced or felt before. The more time you spend getting to know each other, the closer you will become and the deeper your bond will be. It will not take long for you to know that you want to spend the rest of your lives together as husband and wife. You will know that what you have together is genuine love for each other and that you were destined to be together.

One thing that you can be certain of is that you cannot force someone to like you or want to be with you. When connecting with a person, it should be effortless. You both will be on the same page of the same chapter of the same sentence of the same book at the same time. Therefore, you must trust God's timing and know that God will not allow a good thing to pass by you, if you wait on him. The spouse that God has for you will definitely be worth the wait.

Hebrews 11:1 (NLT) says, "Faith is the confidence that what we hope for will actually happen; it gives us assurance about things we cannot see." Sometimes having faith in what we do not see is not easy. However, we can rest in God's goodness and His loving character, trusting that His wisdom is perfect in all things; even when we have to wait. God is always faithful, and He will do just what He says He will do.

Romans 8:25 (NLT) says, "But if we look forward to something we don't yet have, we must wait patiently and confidently." As we wait on God, it does not mean doing nothing or impatiently rushing forward. Instead, we must pray, worship, and enjoy fellowship as we anticipate what God will do. The waiting prepares our heart, mind, and body for what is to come. Trust God and the plans He has for us.

When one is lonely or desperate, they will fall for anything or do anything. Be mindful of who you connect with when you are at a low place in your life. The longing for being accepted by others has always been there. In what or whom have you been striving to gain your value and acceptance? In Genesis 29, Leah understandably yearned for the love of her husband Jacob. However, Jacob loved Leah's sister Rachel more; therefore, Leah never obtained the acceptance she craved from Jacob. After having four sons by Jacob, Leah finally then turned to God to find her significance instead of Jacob. We can try to find our significance in many ways, but only through God can we find our real significance.

I hear you asking the question, "What was God thinking when He created the institution of marriage?" Men and women seem to be totally different from each other, so how are they supposed to come together as husband and wife until death separates them? Well, in the beginning of creation, God said that it was not good for the man to be alone and that He would make a helper who is just right for him. God intended for them to be fruitful and multiply and fill the earth. God never said that marriage would be easy, but we do know that marriage was God's design.

Before you get married, you must know without a shadow of doubt that you want to be married. It has been said that hurt people hurt people. That is why it is so important to heal as individuals prior to getting married because getting married will not heal your brokenness. Do not look for a husband or a wife to complete you. Before you get married, you must already be complete. You were self-sufficient prior to getting married, but with your spouse, the two of you together are a force to be reckoned with.

Society will make marriage look boring or as if it is not fun. Many people have the misconception that you are doomed to a life of misery (the old ball-and-chain image). You may even hear people say that marriage is not all that it is cracked up to be. You have some single people wanting to be married and some married people wanting to be single. However, being married is one of the most amazing things that can happen in your life. Marriage takes work and it takes commitment, and the world needs to see that happy successful marriages do exist.

God did not intend for marriages to be fleeting, which is defined by Oxford Languages as lasting for a very short time or faulting, which is defined by Oxford Languages as the production of a fault or faults. If you are not going to be committed to your marriage until death separates you, then you are at fault. Why not get a dog, cat, or goldfish before you enter a marriage and have no intention of being all in.

People will be on their best behavior in the beginning, but when they are being deceptive, they can only pretend for but so long. Eventually, a person's true character will come out. Therefore, please do not overlook any signs, signals, and warnings. Maya Angelou said if a person shows you who they are, believe them. Are you the same person behind closed doors (in private) and the same when you are in the world (in public)? When you met your spouse, did you allow them to see or get to know the real you, or did you only allow them to see who you thought they wanted you to be, when all along it was an act. You pretended to like the things they liked, and you kept it all together until you got what you wanted (married). Which means that you were being deceptive and got married under false pretenses.

Luke 6:45 (NLT) says, "A good person produces good things from the treasury of a good heart, and an evil person produces evil things from the treasury of an evil heart. What you say flows from what is in your heart." In other words, what is in your heart will come out in what you say and how you act. You will not have to scheme, manipulate or be conniving when you meet the man or woman that God has for you. When Boaz met Ruth, he was not the first man that had the right to marry Ruth according to their customs, but because Boaz was a man of integrity, he went about doing things the right way. Boaz went to the kinsman who initially had the right to redeem Ruth and when this kinsman decided he did not want to marry Ruth, Boaz went about things according to their custom to make Ruth his wife.

When a person is upfront about who they are, they obtain much respect. When my grandmother was living, she would sing a song in church on Sunday morning and a few words of that song that always stuck to me was "be what you are, and live the life, God knows your heart, you can't get by." Jeremiah 17:9–10 (NLT) says, "The human heart is the most deceitful of all things, and desperately wicked. Who really knows how bad it is? But I, the Lord, search all hearts and examine secret motives. I give all people their due rewards, according to what their actions deserve."

When you love a person, you will value and honor them. You will never do or say anything to disrespect them, even when you are upset. Are you able to show your spouse just how committed you are to loving them even when you do not like them? You see a person likes someone because of their qualities, and they love someone in spite of their qualities. Please do not take advantage of a person's love for you.

12

THE WAY GOD INTENDED

Genesis 1:27–28 (NLT) says,

> So God created human being in his own
> image. In the image of God, He created them;
> male and female He created them. Then God
> blessed them and said, "Be fruitful and multiply.
> Fill the earth and govern it. Reign over the fish in
> the sea, the birds in the sky, and all the animals
> that scurry along the ground."

Marriage is ordained of God to protect our lives, give peace, and multiply the earth. God created marriages to be beautiful and there is no relationship between mankind that is greater or more important than marriage.

God went to the earth to make a man but went to the man to make a woman. God felt that Adam needed help to fulfill the vision that He had for him. The foundation of the family is the man, and the woman was intended to rest upon the foundation. Psalm 11:3 (KJV) says, "If the foundations be destroyed, what can the righteous do?" Satan is trying to take the men out and build a foundation with women, but women were not designed to be the foundation.

If the man is unstable or has no relationship with God, then the family starts being unstable. If the family is unstable, then society will be unstable. If society is unstable, then the nation will be unstable. When the husband and wife are connected, then the household will be connected. When the household is connected, then the entire community will be connected. If we want to put this nation back together, then we must put the man back in his rightful place. None of this can happen without God, and we must believe that God will bring the foundation back.

The husband is responsible for his wife. Husbands must make sure their wives are taken care of. The man's job is to know the word of God and the man is supposed to teach the woman. A godly woman must learn to walk with her man to create a family, raise a family, and keep that family together. Godly women must cover their men and help them fulfill their destiny. We must be willing to allow those whom God place in our lives to help us with the call that He has on our life.

Amos 3:3 (KJV) says, "Can two walk together, except they be agreed?" A marriage in which a couple is walking separately is not a marriage the way God intended. In a marriage, you should walk together with common goals in one heart and one mind. You will not be able to be in one heart and mind unless you seek God for his direction and his way. How can you go in the same direction if you are not on the same page? When you said "I do," you both agreed that you were going to walk through life together no matter what came your way. Now what changed?

God knows what is best for us, and we should consult him about every single detail of our life. If you are single and hoping one day to get married, seek God first, and He will bring you the absolute best person that you could marry. Jeremiah 29:11(NLT) reads, "For I know the plans I have for you, says the Lord. They are plans for good and not for disaster, to give you a future and a hope." Although we will not be exempt from pain, suffering, or hardship, God will see us through to a magnificent finish.

Every day will not be sunny in a marriage, but if we did not have some rainy days, we could not appreciate the sunny days. Therefore, you should celebrate every wedding anniversary that you are able to share together because this is a perfect opportunity to reflect on how God brought you through another year together as husband and wife. Since God created marriage, we must understand that marriage only works when we follow the design of the one who created it and know how it is supposed to work.

Harboring negative feelings can only enhance resentment toward your spouse and widen the gap of intimacy. When you love someone, the last thing you want to do is allow anger to manifest. Are you quick to try to make things right or better after a disagreement or do you have a "don't care" attitude? When you genuinely love someone, there should be a sense of urgency and humility to reconcile. Anger is pushed aside and understanding your spouse's feelings becomes a priority. Do you put your spouse's needs and/or desires before your own?

Many people have become fearful of getting married because there does not appear to be many happy successful marriages today. Although there are some couples who have been married for twenty, forty, fifty, and even seventy years, however, they do not appear to be married and in love. Some people get married and have no intention of getting divorced; however, they remain in the marriage, distant from their spouse and sleeping in separate bedrooms. I know this may sound discouraging, but please know that there are still a great number of marriages that do not make it. May I also point out that real love still does exist, and all marriages can be happy and last until death separate you. It is up to each of us to take a stand and fight for our marriages. Let us show the generations to follow what marriage the way God intended is supposed to look like.

Take time to stop and smell the roses on this journey called life. Do not rush through life and take for granted the people and things standing right in front of you. I cannot stress it enough that tomorrow is not promised to anyone. Therefore, spend quality time with your spouse, enjoy your children, and make memories together that will last a lifetime. Simply being present in the home and doing things here, and there is not enough. Have regular date nights with your spouse. Attend your children's school activities, field trips, and after-school activities. Have daily devotion and pray together before the family leaves the home (cover your spouse, your children, and your family daily). Attend worship service together as a family and attend Bible study at church and have Bible study at home together as a family.

Communication is so important and spouses you must communicate with each other daily. Also, you should communicate and interact with your children daily. Not only should you tell your spouse and children how much you love and appreciate them, but you should also show them as well. If you genuinely love your spouse and children, then you will fight for them especially when they are not able to fight for themselves. Do not allow anyone or anything to cause discord in your home. Make sure you are creating a fun-loving atmosphere in your home.

If you are blessed to be married to the kindest, thoughtful, most giving, spiritual spouse who ever lived, then that is your reward. However, I realize that everyone may not have been so blessed to be married to such an amazing spouse. Therefore, if your spouse takes you for granted and you never feel appreciated on this earth, please know that you will receive your reward in heaven. God witnessed you love your spouse even when they did not realize how bless they are to be married to you. Despite this type of treatment, you continued to love them even though you did not get the same love back in return. Regardless of your situation, keep loving, serving, encouraging, and appreciating your spouse. Do not allow yourself to become focused on how well your spouse is loving, serving, encouraging, and appreciating you.

In the book of Hosea, the prophet Hosea experienced betrayal and pain because of his wife's adultery. Hosea 1:2 (NLT) says, "When the Lord first began speaking to Israel through Hosea, he said to him, 'Go and marry a prostitute, so that some of her children will be conceived in prostitution.' This will illustrate how Israel has acted like a prostitute by turning against the Lord and worshiping other gods." Hosea was obedient to God and married Gomer, a prostitute (or promiscuous) woman. God may ask you to do something difficult and extraordinary. If He does, will you be obedient, trusting that His request has a special purpose.

You may be staring the man or woman that God has for you in the face, but because they do not look like what you think they should look like you pass right them. Ladies, he may not be 6'4", 225 lbs., have a six-pack stomach, drive a Mercedes Benz, live in mansion, or have a six- to seven-figure job. Men, she may not cook like your mother, have long hair, the skin complexion you want, or a curvy Coca-Cola-shape body. God will bring you just the person you need. They may not come when you want them to or how you want them, but they will come to you at the right time. Your marriage is a part of God's plan. Do not get weary while waiting on God's best for you.

Good things often take time, and our human nature struggles with patience. Habakkuk 2:3 (NIV) says, "For the revelation awaits an appointed time; it speaks of the end and will not prove false. Though it lingers, wait for it; it will certainly come and will not delay." God prepares every blessing with perfect wisdom and care and it is always worth the wait.

Proverbs 19:21 (NLT) says, "You can make many plans, but the Lord's purpose will prevail." Although planning helps us avoid financial shortcomings, time crunches, and health issues, even the greatest, most thorough strategies cannot eliminate all problems from our lives. God often has a purpose for the trouble He allows into our lives. He may use it to develop patience in us, increase our faith, or bring us closer to Him. When we submit our plans, goals, and hopes to God, He will show us what He wants to accomplish in and through us.

Sometimes we try to fit God into our plans, or we think we know what is best and come up with our way of thinking and doing things. Isaiah 55:8–9 (NIV) says, "For my thoughts are not your thoughts, neither are your ways my ways," declares the Lord. "As the heavens are higher than the earth, so are my ways higher than your ways and my thoughts than your thoughts." We must strive to fit into God's plans. The road may not be easy, but we must trust God in the process.

Even Jesus had to trust God and surrender to His will. While in Gethsemane, prior to his death on the cross, Jesus prayed to God.

Matthew 26:39 (NLT) says, "He went on a little farther and bowed his face to the ground, praying, 'My Father! If it is possible, let this cup of suffering be taken away from me. Yet I want your will to be done, not mine.'" As difficult as it was, God had to go through with His plan to give us a chance to have everlasting life with Him. John 3:16 (NIV) says, "For God so loved the world that He gave His one and only Son, that whoever believes in him shall not perish but have eternal life." How far are you willing to go to express your love for your spouse?

The late British writer and theologian C. S. Lewis wrote a book entitled *The Four Loves*. In this book, he identifies four types of love. The first is agape love, which is considered unconditional "God" love. This type of love is maintained regardless of changing circumstances. C. S. Lewis acknowledges this selfless love as the greatest of the four loves. The next type of love is affection (*storge*). This type of love is described as the most natural, emotive, and widely diffused. It is considered natural because it exists without being forced. It is considered emotive (emotional) because it exists due to affection for someone based off an attachment. It is widely diffused (spread) because it does not focus on those characteristics considered "valuable" or "worthy of love." C. S. Lewis describes this as a dependency-based love that risks destruction if the needs cease to be met.

The third type of love identified by C. S. Lewis is friendship (*philia*). The friendship is the strong bond existing between people who share common values, interests, or activities. The final love is *eros* (romantic love), which, for C. S. Lewis, was love in the sense of "being in love" or "loving" someone. Let us connect the dots to how these four loves can relate to marriages the way God intended. Husbands and wives, you should have unconditional love for each that is able to stand against the storms that will come your way. The love you share with each other must be effortless, and you should express your love for each other daily. Husbands and wives should be each other's best friend and have a bond that is as close as a brother or sister. The love you share with each other must be pure and unbreakable.

It does not feel good to disagree or argue with your spouse. However, when two people are joined together to make one life together, conflict is inevitable. What do you do when you and your spouse do not see eye to eye? You should talk it out. Find a place where you can talk it out. If necessary, find a place to go where you have to behave yourself and where you cannot not get loud with each other (i.e., a restaurant). Write a letter expressing your feelings and share it with each other. Both of you have a right to your own opinion. Remember, you have a mind of your own and you do not always have to agree with your spouse. Just because you do not agree with your spouse, or your spouse does not agree with you that does not mean you no longer love your spouse, or they do not love you. Do not be ready to give your spouse walking papers because they do not always agree with you, or they say something that does not sit well with you.

Philippians 4:6–8 (NLT) says, "Don't worry about anything; instead, pray about everything. Tell God what you need, and thank him for all that he has done. Then you will experience God's peace, which exceeds anything we can understand. His peace will guard your hearts and minds as you live in Christ Jesus. And now, dear brothers and sisters, one final thing. Fix your thoughts on what is true, honorable, and right, and pure, and lovely, and admirable. Think about things that are excellent and worthy of praise."

13

THE TWO SHALL BECOME ONE

In Matthew 19:5–6, while teaching about marriage and divorce, Jesus said, "This explains why a man leaves his father and mother and is joined to his wife, and the two are united into one. Since they are no longer two but one, let no one split apart what God has joined together." God joins a husband and a wife into a one-flesh union. This union is the heart of what marriage is. Have you ever tried to tear apart something that was joined together by the strongest adhesive? Well, when marriages are torn apart, it affects not just the couple, but if children are involved, they are affected, the extended families are affected, mutual friends, finances, careers, and living situations are all affected.

The words "I love you" have been misused for so long that many people are afraid to get marry or will enter marriage lightly. Marriage is not always seen as a sacred union between one man and one woman who serve one another until death separates them. What is often called love is nothing more than a selfish desire. Many married couples live together selfishly. They have not forgone their personal freedom and opened their hearts to love each other unconditionally. True marital joy comes from giving ourselves in love to another person. Real love not only seeks to give, but also longs to unite. Therefore, a happy successful marriage requires sacrifice and faithfulness.

First Corinthians 13:4–7 (NLT) show us what real love looks like. It states that love is patient and kind. Love is not jealous or boastful or proud or rude. It does not demand its own way. It is not irritable and keeps no record of being wronged. It does not rejoice about injustice but rejoices whenever the truth wins out. Love never gives up, never loses faith, is always hopeful, and endures through every circumstance. Now that is love, and we all should seek to demonstrate this type of love. It will take both of you as one to make your marriage work.

Genesis 29 tells of a story about Jacob and Rachel. Jacob met Rachel and Laban, her father, and stayed and worked for Laban for about a month when Laban told Jacob that he should not work for him without pay just because they were relatives. Laban told Jacob to tell him how much his wages should be. Laban had two daughters, Leah and Rachel. There was no sparkle in Leah's eyes, but Rachel had a beautiful figure and lovely face. Since Jacob was in love with Rachel, he told her father that he would work for him for seven years if he would give Rachel as his wife.

Laban agreed and Jacob worked seven years to pay for Rachel. When the time came for Jacob to marry Rachel, Laban brought Leah to Jacob instead. When Jacob woke up the next morning and realized that it was Leah instead of Rachel, he went to Laban and questioned what he had done. Laban told Jacob that it is not their custom for the younger daughter to get married before the older daughter, but if he worked another seven years for him, then he will give him Rachel too. Jacob agreed and worked another seven years for Laban and eventually married Rachel. As you can see Jacob had an unbelievable love for Rachel.

During creation, God knew that it would not be good for the man to be alone, so he made a helper that would be just right for the man. Ecclesiastes 4:9–12 (NLT) says, "Two people are better than one, for they can help each other succeed. If one person falls, the other can reach out and help. A person standing alone can be attacked and defeated, but two can stand back-to-back and conquer. Three are even better, for a triple-braided cord is not easily broken." The three cords represent a husband, a wife and God. These three form a close relationship that is not easily broken. Therefore, I encourage you to invite God into your marriage as that third chord.

A marriage requires 100 percent, and you must give yourself wholeheartedly to your spouse. First, give your whole heart to God, and then give your whole heart to your spouse. Your spouse wants your heart when it comes to time, building a home together, working together as a team, when it comes to money and saving together. Be generous with your time, affection, and abilities. You were born with special abilities, and you have something that your spouse needs or wants, and your spouse has something that you need or want. Use your abilities to bless your spouse. There is a purpose for your marriage.

Genesis 2:21–24 (NLT) says,

> So the Lord God caused the man to fall into a deep sleep. While the man slept, the Lord God took out one of the man's ribs and closed up the opening. Then the Lord God made a woman from the rib, and he brought her to the man. "At last!" the man exclaimed. "This one is bone from my bone, and flesh from my flesh! She will be called woman because she was taken from man. This explains why a man leaves his father and mother and is joined to his wife, and the two are united into one.

The sexual union between a husband and wife demonstrates the physical expression of the leaving, cleaving, and becoming one flesh. God's plan of one, is one God, one man, one woman, one marriage, one sex partner, one flesh, one lifetime. When a couple becomes one flesh, they demonstrate the sacred commitment between a husband and wife and show what it means to stand together as one against every storm that may come their way, until death separates them.

When some couples get married, they choose to include a unity ceremony during their wedding. Some common unity ceremonies are the unity candle, the unity sand ceremony, and the salt covenant ceremony. Unity ceremonies symbolizes the joining of two individuals coming together in marriage. Many times, a unity ceremony include other family members to represent two families joining together. The unity candle ceremony is when couples getting married light one large candle from two smaller candles. Typically, the smaller candles are lit by the mothers of the bride and groom, which represents the merging of two families. The unity sand ceremony is when a couple getting married pours sand from separate receptacles into a shared one. The sand ceremony is very powerful for blended families with children as it is a visual perception demonstrating the coming together of two groups becoming one. A marriage salt covenant is when the couple getting married pours salt from individual receptacles into a shared receptacle. This demonstrates how their commitment to each other cannot be broken unless they each can retrieve their own grains of salt. Therefore, since this is impossible, it symbolizes an unbreakable covenant and vow of eternal love.

The purpose of marriage is oneness. You cannot become one flesh if you are selfish. When you are selfish, you can become insensitive and that it not the way a marriage should be. When your spouse is hurting, you are hurting. What is a top priority to your spouse, should also be a top priority for you. Becoming one is a life journey, and God must be the center of your life and your marriage. Pray individually, intercede on behalf of your spouse, pray together, and lift up your spouse. God wants to give you everything you need for your marriage.

When you get married, you must make a move from a single mindset to a married mindset. You may have felt like you could not depend on anyone else before, and even if you were in a relationship with someone, you were the one doing everything. You must move from that "lone ranger" mindset to a "two shall become one" mindset. Remember, in marriage you were not joined together to do this alone. You are in this together as husband and wife until death separates you. Now make sure you have a couple's mindset, married mindset, and "sharing your life with someone else" mindset.

Song of Songs 6:3 (NLT) says, "I am my lover's, and my lover is mine. He browses among the lilies." In this verse, it is being expressed how the couple belong to each other. It is only in marriage that two people unite and become one in mind, body, and heart.

When you love someone, you will do everything you can to make sure they are safe, well taken care of, and have all they need, even if it means making personal sacrifices to care for them.

Communicating love and expressing admiration in words and actions can enhance every marriage. Husbands let your wife know how much you adore her and reassure her that there is nobody else you would rather be married to. Wives, let your husband know how much you admire him and grateful to be his wife. As time continues to pass and couples become more comfortable with each other, a marriage can start to lose that initial spark. You no longer look at each other like you used to or you do not touch each other the way you use to. When things seem to spiral downward, you start to focus on the negative. Instead of focusing on the negative, focus on the positive and remember all those good memories you shared together. As a matter of fact, create new memories and explore some new things together.

Romans 8:35 (NIV) says, "Who shall separate us from the love of Christ? Shall trouble or hardship or persecution or famine or nakedness or danger or sword?" No, none of these things will be able to separate us from God's love. Therefore, please do not allow anything to separate you from your spouse. Hard times will come, but instead of hard times tearing you apart, allow hard times to bring you closer together.

The goal after every disagreement you have with your spouse is to make it to the other side together. Many people do not know how to bounce back after a disagreement. They do not know what to do, what to say, or how to approach the other person. Although things may seem very awkward, please do not allow time to keep you apart. The enemy will use that time to play with your mind, get in your thoughts, keep you reliving, or replaying every detail of your argument, therefore, trying to keep you upset with each other.

Let it all go and move forward so you can get pass that incident. Please do not allow it to fester or linger in it because the enemy does not want to see your marriage prosper. Fight for your marriage and make every effort to get to the other side of that incident. Ephesians 4:26–27 (NIV) says, "'In your anger do not sin.' Do not let the sun go down while you are still angry, and do not give the devil a foothold." Therefore, you have until midnight to resolve your conflict. Let your spouse know that you know they love you because love covers a lot of things, and you are so glad that they made the effort and took the time so that you both could get to the other side of that disagreement together.

Please be certain that you deal with *all* of the issues that come your way because you do not want to leave any room for Satan to come in and divide you. Also, make sure that you are being honest with your spouse and being real with yourself. When you do not express your true feelings, then you allow room for bitterness, resentment, and animosity to set in and Satan will take that and run with it. Also, it would not be good for one spouse to think that everything is going well in the marriage while the other spouse is actually still harboring ill feelings. You must acknowledge what you are feeling and ask God to help you replace those feelings with a sweet, joyful spirit. We can become better at resolving conflict as the Holy Spirit produces self-control, gentleness, and patience within us. We should be able to settle all disagreements peacefully with our spouse.

God is greater than any problem that we can or will face in our marriage. God can bring good out of our most difficult circumstances and help us get to the other side of any issue and experience love, joy, peace, and happiness with each other. I know the good times always looks better than not so good times, and we would prefer not to experience difficult times in our marriages. However, just like in 2 Corinthians 12, Paul experienced difficulty and prayed and asked God three times to remove the thorn in his flesh; however, each time God told him that "My grace is all you need. My power works best in weakness" (verses 8–9). God's grace is enough to get you to the other side of your challenges His way.

Can you forgive your spouse after they have let you down? Will you exercise enough grace when they have been convicted on how they treated you? Tom Eyen wrote the song "And I Am Telling You I'm Not Going," which has been sung by Jennifer Holliday and

Jennifer Hudson. Some of the lyrics in this song says: "And I am tellin' you, I'm not goin. Even though the rough times are showin'. There's just no way. Darlin there's no way I'm livin without you." Are you going to stand by the commitment you made on your wedding day to have and to hold, for better, for worse, for richer, for poorer, in sickness and in health, to love and cherish until death separates you?

14

A Sustainable Marriage

According to *Oxford Dictionary, sustainable* means able to be maintained at a certain rate or level. *Meriam-Webster Dictionary* defines *sustained* as maintained at length without interruption or weakening, lasting, prolonged. Since God intended for marriage to last until death separate you, what does it take to have a sustainable marriage?

One thing you must do to have a sustainable marriage is have intense love for each other. Song of Songs 8:6–7 (NLT) says,

> Place me like a seal over your heart, like a seal on your arm. For love is as strong as death, its jealousy as enduring as the grave. Love flashes like fire, the brightest kind of flame. Many waters cannot quench love, nor can rivers drown it. If a man tried to buy love with all his wealth his offer would be utterly scorned. Love is priceless and even the richest person cannot buy it.

First Corinthians 13:4–7 shows us the way God wants us to love. The New International Version says,

> Love is patient, love is kind. It does not envy, it does not boast, it is not proud. It does not dishonor others, it is not self-seeking, it is

not easily angered, it keeps no record of wrongs. Love does not delight in evil but rejoices with the truth. It always protects, always trusts, always hopes, always perseveres.

Ask yourself am I patient with my spouse? Does my spouse consider me to be a kind person? Do I brag about what I do for my spouse? Am I able to humble myself and lay my pride aside for the betterment of our marriage? Am I doing anything to bring dishonor to my marriage? Am I considerate of my spouse's feelings, interest, needs, desires, and preferences? Am I slow to get angry or do I lose my temper easily? Do I hold grudges or am I able to forgive and forget?

Another thing you must do to have a sustainable marriage is to be forgiving. People are not perfect and are bound to make mistakes. You must show forgiveness for truly repentant mistakes and not hold grudges. You should not throw up past mistakes to hurt or punish each other. Colossians 3:13 (NLT) says, "Make allowance for each other's faults, and forgive anyone who offends you. Remember, the Lord forgave you, so you must forgive others." Love is evident when you can forgive each other and still love each other after feeling offended or disappointed.

Not going to bed angry is one more thing you must do to have a sustainable marriage. Ephesians 4:26–27 (NLT) says, "'Don't sin by letting anger control you.' Don't let the sun go down while you are still angry, for anger gives a foothold to the devil." Work out your issues instead of using the silent treatment or allow your frustration to grow. James 1:19–20 (NIV) says, "My dear brothers and sisters, take note of this: Everyone should be quick to listen, slow to speak and slow to become angry, because human anger does not produce the righteousness that God desires."

Communication is said to be one of the main ingredients to a successful marriage. It is so important that you communicate your feelings, needs, thoughts, frustrations, plans, and ideas with your spouse frequently. When you communicate effectively with your spouse daily, then your bond can grow deeper, and you can grow closer to each other. Arguing can be considered a form of communication; however, communication is not you trying to prove your point. Proving your point will not save your marriage. When you genuinely love your spouse, you will fight for them and your marriage. You will protect them and your marriage. You will fight for your marriage when things get tough.

Some people may feel that because they are in their twenties, thirties, forties, or even fifties that they do not need anyone else. You make a lot of money, obtained the house of your dreams, and drive a nice car. However, what good is that dream house, fancy car, or large bank account if you do not have someone to visit your home, ride in that nice car or enjoy that money with. Please believe that by the time you get into your sixties, seventies, eighties, or even nineties you will be praying that you had someone in that house with you who could help you, who loves you and care about you. Statistics show that people who are married, live longer, are healthier and is more financially stable. More importantly, God did not intend for us to be alone.

God wants us to be in a marriage that is successful and that is evident by love, honor, respect, and fun. Are you loving your spouse the way they need to be loved? Are you honoring the vows that you made to each other before God and your witnesses? Are you demonstrating mutual respect? Are you making sure you have fun together?

Proverbs 17:22 (NLT) says, "A cheerful heart is good medicine, but a broken spirit saps a person's strength." Now you see, laughter really is good for the soul. Keeping laughter as a part of your marriage is a way to sustain your marriage. Do not be so serious all the time. Be silly, take silly photos, dance, let the kid inside of you out, go to an amusement park, play games, and laugh a lot.

What connects you as husband and wife should not be how good he or she looks, how much money he or she has or even how good the sex is. God created sex, and it should be cherished and enjoyed between a husband and wife as the good gift that it is. However, a sustainable marriage is not made by having sex. You can have all the sex you want with your spouse, and he or she can still walk out of the door. If you want to have a sustainable marriage, you must be loyal to your spouse. Be committed to remain faithful to your spouse in body and in mind. You show deep respect to your spouse when you remain faithful to them. Loyalty builds trust, shows love, and allows you to stay connected to your spouse and family.

Feelings are not enough to sustain a marriage. Emotions come and go. Your emotional state can change from being happy to sad, being at peace to being angry, being satisfied to feeling disappointed. Relationships will go through hard times, changing times and even strange times. Do not rely on your emotions; instead rely on the Holy Spirit that dwells within you. Your feelings cannot control your destiny. Therefore, do not allow other people or situations to manipulate your feelings.

Philippians 1:9 (NLT) says, "I pray that your love will overflow more and more, and that you will keep on growing in knowledge and understanding." Prior to being crucified on the cross, Jesus commanded his disciples to love one another. John 13:34 (NLT) says, "So now I am giving you a new commandment: Love each other. Just as I have loved you, you should love each other." When you and your spouse are able to look beyond each other's faults, you will be able to extend love to each other, even during emotional moments in your marriage. Remember, mutual love a key ingredient to a happy, healthy marriage that will last until death separates you.

When you have a sustainable marriage, you demonstrate for generations to follow how to have a sustainable marriage. The word love has been watered down and often has no true value. An authentic way of demonstrating what it means to love and cherish is needed for the generations to follow. When you cherish your spouse, you lift them up, you exalt them, and you adore them. A healthy marriage needs to be seen and when people see a healthy marriage, they can see God.

The questions to ask yourself now is, what am I doing to sustain my marriage? Am I nurturing my marriage? Well, if you want your marriage to improve you should not ask your spouse to improve; instead, you should improve and then your marriage will improve. How might your marriage change if serving and worshiping God together was a priority? Make sure that your marriage is built on a sure foundation and that sure foundation is Jesus Christ. When Jesus is the cornerstone of your relationship, you will have a fruitful, sturdy, steadfast, unmovable, always abounding in the work and word of God marriage.

Trust is a part of the foundation for a successful marriage and trust begins with commitment. To have a sustainable marriage, each spouse must be totally committed to each other and the marriage. What can you do to show your spouse that you are committed to the vows that you made to each other? How can you secure your marriage? Remember, love never gives up, therefore, no matter what, divorce should not be an option. Gospel duo Mary Mary has a song titled "Can't Give Up Now." In this song, they remind us that there will be mountains, that we will have to climb and battles that we will have to fight. Nobody told us the road would be easy, but I don't believe God brought us this far to leave us. Never said there wouldn't be trials, never said we wouldn't fall, never said that everything would go the way we want it to go, but when we feel as if all hope is gone, just lift our head up to the sky and say help me to be strong.

Every marriage will have challenges; however, these challenges should not destroy a marriage. Remember, there is no challenge to hard for God. Both of you must be all in and put in 100 percent to work through problems that arise in your marriage. Instead of fighting with your spouse, fight for your spouse and fight for your marriage. Being married requires you to be totally and exclusively committed to each other. Do not waste any more time by allowing problems or conflict to ruin your ability to enjoy God's gift of marriage. Your marriage must continue to grow after your wedding day.

If your marriage is need of restoration, have you asked God to restore your marriage? Whatever you are dealing with in your marriage is not too big or small for God. Do you believe that God can heal your marriage? Well I encourage you to trust God's process and His timing. Proverbs 21:1 (KJV) says, "The king's heart is in the hand of the Lord, as the rivers of water: he turneth it whithersoever he will." This reminds us that that God is in control. While you wait on God to handle your situation His way, remember Psalm 46:10, which says, "Be still, and know that I am God!" Take time each day to be still and honor God.

If you think your spouse or your marriage is boring or if you think your sex life is dull, please know that it takes more than love to make a marriage work. Love will be tested, love will get weary, and love will be offended. However, when hard times come, you must realize that there is something far greater and much deeper than love. It is purpose. There is a divine purpose for God bringing you and your spouse together as husband and wife. You may have made a mistake and you may have tried to do things your way. Now you have a choice. You can continue to do things your way or you can choose to do things God's way. Which way are you going to choose? I suggest that you spend more time in prayer instead of just giving up. Therefore, you must fight for the destiny of your marriage. Fight for the destiny of your family. Ask God for divine intervention. Trust me, it will change your life, and it will change your marriage.

15

DON'T GET CAUGHT IN THE TRAP

Proverbs 7:10–27 warns young men about immoral women. Although the warning is geared toward young men, it applies to everyone whether you are young, old, male or female. It is important to recognize strategies of temptation and run away from them swiftly. Let us look at some of the strategies the woman in these scriptures used. Proverbs 7:10 (NLT) reads, "The woman approached him, seductively dressed and sly of heart." In this verse, the woman is dressed to lure men. It is okay to want to look good. As a matter of fact, you should want to dress nice for your spouse; however, you should always be mindful of your motive when it comes to trying to impress or look good for others.

Proverbs 7:13 reads, "She threw her arms around him and kissed him." In this verse, the woman is very bold. Some people do not care whether you are married or not. Even some who are married do not honor their vows and will make all the first moves. In Proverbs 7:16–18, the woman invites the young man over to her place. Verse 16–18 reads, "My bed is spread with beautiful blankets, with colored sheets of Egyptian linen. I've perfumed my bed with myrrh, aloes, and cinnamon. Come, let's drink our fill of love until morning. Let's enjoy each other's caresses."

In a very deceitful way, the woman responds to the young man's objection. Proverbs 7:19–20 reads, "For my husband is not home. He's away on a long trip. He has taken a wallet full of money with him and won't return until later this month." In Proverbs 7:21 reads, "So she seduced him with her pretty speech and enticed him with her flattery." The woman then uses smooth talk to persuade the young man. Then finally she traps him. Proverbs 7:22–23 says, "He followed her at once, like an ox going to the slaughter. He was like a stag caught in a trap, awaiting the arrow that would pierce its heart. He was like a bird flying into a snare, little knowing it would cost him his life."

There are consequences and repercussions to your decisions, and you will be held accountable for what you decide. Sex is one of God's good gifts, but when we seek it outside of marriage, it is like an ox going to the slaughter. Sin can be alluring and addicting, but it always ends in death. There are steps you can take to avoid sexual sins. For one, you can guard your mind. Do not read books, look at pictures, movies, etc., that will stimulate wrong desires.

Second, stay away from places and people that will tempt you to sin. Third, do not just think about that moment. Instead, think about the future, the risks, and the consequences. A moment of thrill or pleasure can lead to a future of ruins. You may think you can get away with what you are doing or even think what your spouse do not know cannot hurt them. However, you are sadly mistaken.

Hebrews 4:13 (NLT) reminds us that nothing in all creation is hidden from God. Everything is naked and exposed before his eyes, and he is the one to whom we are accountable. God sees and knows all we do and think. We cannot hide anything from God. However, despite our shortcomings, God still loves us. He wants us to confess our sins, repent of them (turn from them) and walk rightly with him. James 5:16 (NLT) says, "Confess your sins to each other and pray for each other so that you may be healed. The earnest prayer of a righteous person has great power and produces wonderful results."

As a married couple, confess your faults to each other so that you may be healed. Whether it is repenting to your spouse for getting angry, having unforgiveness or for doing something wrong. Humble yourself and confess your sins. Do not give the devil anything to make you feel guilty about or any reason to make you lie to your spouse. Do not give the devil any secrets for you to cover/hide or any lustful behavior to tempt you with or any thoughts to play with your mind. Not only should you be real, open, and honest with your spouse, but also be real, open, and honest with yourself. Do not leave any room for the devil to have the upper hand over you.

Be mindful of what you are doing to hold onto people from your past or even attract new people. As you know, people can be persuasive and will try to lure you to be unfaithful to your spouse. If you are the pursuer, please find the strength to stop what you are doing. Adultery is a trap and not only is it dangerous, but it is also painful and cause damage to everyone involved. Infidelity leads to mistrust. While fidelity leads to trust. Joy and happiness in a marriage comes from faithfulness and loyalty.

According to *Merriam-Webster Dictionary*, in a relationship, being faithful means that you refrain from investing romantically in others. Being faithful means you give your love, respect, and attention to your partner. You honor fidelity and you do not have sex with another person. Being loyal means to stand by someone in good times and bad. You defend them and you support them.

Many people only apologize about being unfaithful when they get caught. Which then leaves the other person questioning if it is really a genuine apology. It has been said that confession is good for the soul. Healing can come from owning your shortcomings. Own your mistakes and wrongdoings. Acknowledge, accept, deal with it, and own what you did. Do not try to blame, manipulate, or deceive your spouse. Do not try to make your spouse out to be the bad person or feel as if they were the one who did something wrong when you were the one who was unfaithful, the one who was not honest and betrayed their trust.

Be upfront and honest with your spouse no matter how difficult it may be. Pray and ask the Holy Spirit to give you strength to confess your wrongdoings. Your spouse can handle the truth better than having to deal with the hurt from your dishonesty. Allow your spouse the opportunity to decide on their own what they want to do next versus you assuming you already know how they are going to react. You are sadly mistaken when you make that assumption and decide not to be honest or upfront with your spouse because you thought it was the best thing to do. There is a saying, "Tell the truth and shame the devil." Do not give the devil anything to use against you, hold over your head, destroy your marriage, or divide your family.

Please note that you are only asking for problems when you try to hold onto past relationships. You leave the door wide open for Satan to play on your spouse's mind when you are holding on to a relationship you do not have to have. If you do not let go of these past relationships in the beginning, you leave room for Satan to test you. Sex is a great thing in the context that God created it to be (between husband and wife). However, sex has been distorted from God's intention. Everything that God said was good, Satan finds a way to corrupt it. John 10:10 (NLT) says, "The thief's purpose is to steal and kill and destroy. My purpose is to give them a rich and satisfying life."

Adam and Eve formed the first institution of marriage. They were living in paradise without a care in the world. Then here comes the snake (temptation) and life in paradise for them was no longer the same because they gave into that temptation. Even though that temptation will be there, your response must be different. Being unfaithful is a decision. Your real strength is shown when you can be unfaithful, but you choose not to. It is understandable that you may see another man or woman whom you may find attractive. You are human and you have eyes; however, when you do not pursue, follow, or act on anything after that initial look, then you win.

Do not get caught in the trap for you stand to lose everything (your spouse, your family, your reputation, your career). Is that moment of thrill worth it? Do not take your spouse for granted and remember that if you want favor from God, then you must honor your marriage. Proverbs 18:22 (NIV) says, "He who finds a wife finds what is good and receives favor from the Lord." When you find your good thing, cherish it. Quartet group Doc McKenzie and Hi-Lites have a song entitled "Hold on to What You've Got," and in this song, he sings about how the grass is not greener on the other side; it just looks that way. He encourages both men and women to hold on to their spouse. What now may seem old to you will be brand new to someone else.

Respect marriage when you are single because you do not want to experience the same thing you inflicted onto someone else when or if you get married. When you know someone is married be very cautious of how you befriend them. Also be aware of your motives when voicing an opinion or being critical about the spouse of someone of the opposite sex you consider yourself friends with. I'm sure some of you reading this book at some point in your life may have had someone of the opposite sex that you considered your best friend. I will not say all, but many platonic friendships do not remain platonic. Either one of you or both of you develop feelings for the other person that are stronger than wanting to be "just friends." However, you are not honest about those feelings that developed over the duration of your friendship. You may have dated other people or even gotten married to someone else, but those feelings did not go away. Some people have said things like well my spouse knows all about my friend of the opposite sex or my friend of the opposite sex knows all about my spouse and my kids call them uncle or auntie. Now let's keep it real. Does your spouse (or if you are not married the person you are in relationship with) know about the time when you kissed your best friend of the opposite sex or about the time that you had sex with them or about the true feelings that you really have for them?

Some people are convinced that men and women can be "just friends." Regardless of what you believe, I do not think that it is wise for a woman to have a man (other than her husband) as her best friend and vice versa for a man to have a woman (other than his wife) as his best friend. Truth be told, I do not think it is wise to be communicating with someone of the opposite sex when you are in a relationship with someone and definitely not when you are married. If you and your spouse share mutual friends, it will be because you are friends with the spouse who is the same sex as you. Do not disrespect their marriage and develop a closer bond with the spouse who is of opposite sex from you by having conversations, meals, or hanging out outside of your time together as couples.

Statistics reveal that nearly half of all marriages will end in divorce. However, despite these alarming results, every marriage has a 100 percent chance of surviving and being happy. Couples can unlearn the behaviors that predict divorce and destroy love by replacing them with behaviors that keep their love alive. Couples must learn how to rise above those petty things that try to pull you apart. Respect each other's likes and dislikes, opinions and beliefs, hopes, and dreams and fears even though you may not always understand them.

People will come up with all kinds of excuses regarding why they were unfaithful to their spouse such as loss of interest, lust, insecurities, and lack of self-discipline. Whether you were married one year or fifty years, please do not fall into the trap and think that the grass will be greener on the other side. Instead, hold on to the spouse that you have and strive to spice things up in your own marriage. Please note that spicing things up in your marriage does not mean that you need to be swingers, have an open marriage, threesome, or foursome.

Society has adapted to the idea that anything other than a monogamous marriage is acceptable. However, I must warn you that it is not acceptable and never will be acceptable according to God's purpose for marriage. It should not be acceptable for your spouse to have sex with someone else, even though you agree or state that you will always be open with each other about being involved with someone. Trust me, at some point, that will backfire. One or both of you may have only agreed to this option because you thought that was what the other person really wanted or that was the only way to save your marriage or figured one person was already being unfaithful so why not be open about it instead of being sneaky about it.

There should not be any secrets in your marriage. Technology and the use of social media has found a way to wreak havoc in marriages. You find some people sending direct or private messages on social media and see people accessing pornography on the internet. Then some people will have emotional affairs when they allow themselves to get emotionally attached to someone other than their spouse whether it is through conversations over the phone, in person, texting or sexting. Inappropriate relationships are now common in the work force. When you start spending time with someone on the job (your work husband/wife) by eating lunch together every day, discussing your marital problems, flirting, or even engaging in any type of intimacy (holding hands, hugging, kissing, sex), you have defiled your marriage bed.

Hebrews 13:4 (NIV) says, "Marriage should be honored by all, and the marriage bed kept pure, for God will judge the adulterer and all the sexually immoral." Therefore, if there are passwords to social media accounts, computers, email accounts, cell phones, share them with your spouse and demonstrate to them that you do not have anything to hide. Do not go and get a second cell phone to sneak and have inappropriate communication with someone else or try to delete inappropriate messages prior to your spouse finding them to make it look as if you are not doing something when you really are. Remember, you cannot hide anything from God and what is done in the dark will eventually come to the light.

Sex was God's idea as a gift to husbands and wives. God's plan is for us to have a healthy marriage that includes a healthy sex life. Some of you may have grown up thinking that sex is sinful, bad, or even shameful. Some of you may have had some bad experiences with sex/sexual activities due to molestation or rape. Whatever your situation may have been, I strongly encourage you to be open to God's healing because God can heal your brokenness.

Love and respect can help build intimacy, while disrespect interrupts the flow of romance. Get to know your spouse and learn their sexual needs/desires as well as what turns them on. Create an environment for sexual activity. Talk romantically to each other, hug, cuddle, kiss and of course, make passionate love to your spouse. Sex has a physical, emotional, relational, and spiritual side (one flesh). Be creative and create romantic moments with your spouse. Get away for the weekend and continue dating your spouse. Keep pursuing your spouse and remain devoted to each other. Let your spouse know that you need them, you want them, and the two of you are in this together. One person cannot make a marriage work alone.

When a marriage is built on real love, there is no fear of deception, manipulation, or exploitation. True love is not fickle, which means that it is not here today and gone tomorrow. True love is everlasting, which means that it endures until death separates you. Are you devoted and committed to an everlasting love with your spouse? Are you trusting God to sustain your marriage? Are you trusting God to protect your marriage? Then declare today no weapon that is formed against you or your marriage shall prosper.

ABOUT THE AUTHOR

Dr. Nicole Witherspoon was born in Manning, South Carolina, and is a 1995 graduate of Manning High School. After completing high school, she attended South Carolina State University and graduated cum laude with a bachelor's degree in social work in May of 1999.

Dr. Witherspoon continued her graduate studies at the University of South Carolina in Columbia, South Carolina, and graduated cum laude with a master's degree in social work in May of 2000. It has always been a desire for Dr. Witherspoon to earn the highest degree possible, and she accomplished that goal by successfully graduating cum laude with a doctor of philosophy degree in marriage and family therapy from Amridge University in Montgomery, Alabama, in June of 2015. Dr. Witherspoon has gained extensive experience as a licensed social worker in healthcare in the areas of behavioral health, dialysis, hospitals, home health care, and home hospice. Dr. Witherspoon is the owner of Dr. Nicole's Marriage & Family Enrichment Services, LLC, which is dedicated to healing broken marriages, broken families, and hurting individuals.

As a Christian, Dr. Witherspoon penned this book providing tools and resources to heal marriages. Dr. Witherspoon was awarded Young Woman of the Year by the Concerned Black Clergy of Atlanta in 2003, and The Winnie Hohn Christian Counseling Award in 2015. Dr. Witherspoon enjoys cooking, spending time with her family and traveling. Dr. Witherspoon currently reside in Summerville, South Carolina.

CPSIA information can be obtained
at www.ICGtesting.com
Printed in the USA
BVHW031458230123
656904BV00005B/35